"What do girls do who haven't any mothers to help them through their troubles?" – **Louisa May Alcott**

I'll let you in on a little secret. I wasn't always sure what good was or much less how to be good. So here's what I did: I pretended that I was a Mama and had a daughter of my own. If I didn't want my daughter to do something, then I would not do it myself. It was so simple that way. And that is how I taught myself to be proper. There was only so much my Daddy could say and do about certain topics. The rest would be up to me to figure out.

THE WOMAN OF THE HOUSE

AMANDA M. HARDING

A MEMOIR

Cover by Meg Hamilton of Rodeo Co. Photography

In loving memory of my beautiful and courageous mother. You are with me always. Little Vivienne-June knows all about and loves her sweet Grandma dearly. I'm so grateful for your unconditional love.

Author's Note

The Woman of the House is a memoir. The names of the characters have been changed for privacy purposes. This memoir is a collection of personal memories during a pivotal time in my young adult life. I believe we remember things the way we need to remember them, and thus, not all details may be entirely accurate.

THE WOMAN OF THE HOUSE

Prologue

I am sometimes reminded that "weird" things are actually "God" things. In junior high, I had an English teacher who encouraged us to submit entries to a writing contest sponsored by the local newspaper. It just so happened that when I went home that night, the house was dark and empty. It was especially lonely, and I broke down crying, remembering my Mama. I sat in the bathroom with a legal notepad, and I just began writing and writing and writing. I cried, and I let myself cry some more. I did not lift the pencil from the paper for three hours. The result was the most sincere piece of writing I ever drafted. The next morning I read what I wrote, and I realized that I wanted to share my story. I never said anything to my teacher. I just placed it in a folder on his desk. A few weeks later he came up to me after class and told me that I had won some sort of Gold Key award. He handed me a certificate and a little gold pin. We were both equally surprised. But that piece of writing just flowed from me uncontrollably. And somebody else actually liked it. How weird.

This acceptance, this reward of knowing that someone must have enjoyed reading my writing — it made me feel joyful. Mama had a way of making me feel joyful about my creative side. I've rarely experienced a parallel joy in any other endeavor since Mama died. I had a feeling this writing thing was an avenue I would need to tap into. For many years, however, I could not for the life of me figure out what my story was. I did not understand why God blessed me with a gift without telling me how to use it. Then one day it dawned on me that God had indeed given me a story.

Amanda M. Harding

The Woman of the House

Amanda M. Harding

Part One
THE END

The Woman of the House

APPEARANCES

With the palm of my hand, I pushed aside the strands of hair that were matted to the salty ribbons streaming down my cheeks. I felt as though I had fallen into a deep sleep, eyes wide open, in a pool of chlorine. I squinted enough to see a swollen sky outside the window. The neighborhood gave off an eerie silence, and I watched as rain dripped steadily from the gutter above. Closing my eyes did nothing to soothe the incessant burning. I carefully fingered the tiny balls of cotton on the almost threadbare sheets. Slowly, I recognized that these were not the overly starched pale green sheets I had become accustomed to. Suddenly, severely, my heart throbbed. My eyes ached. My stomach convulsed. I knew what today was. I tried. I tried so hard to wish I had never woken up. Today would be the third day I lived without my Mama.

Overtaken by numbness, I fixated on the JC Penney bag abandoned on my white dresser, then on the nail polish stain that Mama had desperately tried to scrub out of the carpet. I thought she would be so mad when I told her about the spill, but to my relief, she wasn't. The night before, Cindy had taken me shopping. She seemed sincere enough, but I knew. I knew she felt some sort of unexplainable pride in her role in all of this. I knew she must like my Daddy now. He was back on the market, after all. I would have to keep my eyes on her. She would be viewed as a savior, taking care of the little motherless girl. I hadn't been shopping in months.

At the department store, I recognized so many outfits that my friends' Moms had recently bought for them. While reciting the Pledge of Allegiance each morning, I would stand at my desk with my hand over my heart and silently envy my friends' new clothing.

I pushed aimlessly through the racks of clothing, not exactly sure what it was that we were looking for, while Cindy whispered to the nosey saleslady. They caught me off guard when they returned my glance, so I innocently held up a lacy pink sweater for Cindy's approval.

Cindy had a daughter of her own who was several years older than me. She was always dressed in popular fashions. I had seen a picture of her on their fireplace mantel in which she was wearing a similar pink sweater, her arms wrapped around her younger brother. I supposed that if Cindy thought it was good enough for her daughter, she would be impressed with my taste as well.

The saleslady blushed. It was not a sympathetic blush. Instead, it made me blush with embarrassment. With saddened eyes, Cindy hurried over to me, placing her French manicured hand on my back, and ushered me to another section of the store. She took the hanger from my grip and discarded it haphazardly on a shelf where it didn't belong. After swiftly pushing through several racks of clothing, she settled on a black velvet button-up blouse that had a silver collar paired with an ankle-length black velvet skirt.

Cindy held the outfit up to my body and carefully studied the combination. I pursed my lips as thoughts flew through my head. Mama would never have picked that out. She always told me black was not my color.

As I buttoned the last button on the blouse that I swore I would never wear again, I made my way on to the carpeted hallway and into the bathroom. The hallway was empty. Thank God. I could hear the familiar hum of Daddy's electric razor, and I could smell the scent of Royal Copenhagen. I admired the two new paintings Mama had recently hung in the bathroom.

The overhead lights scorched my parched eyes, as did my reflection. I pulled open the top drawer of the vanity and reached all the way in the back until I retrieved a little triangle makeup sponge and several other items. I quickly dotted the brown creamy liquid around my eyes, desperate to conceal my swollen eyelids. I had seen Mama do this.

I had taken these items from Mama's hospital bathroom. She hadn't touched her makeup bag in months, and I knew if I did not salvage them, they would be soon discarded by an unknowing nurse. I read in a teen magazine that it was crucial to blend the makeup around your jawline so that you did not look like you were wearing a mask. I double- and triple-checked my jawline. I didn't want anyone to notice such a faux pas. Next, I applied a metal, scissor-like contraption to my dark lashes and squeezed down hard. When I released the contraption, my lashes practically touched my eyebrows.

I was now the woman of the house. And my first royal appearance would take place on this dreadful morning. I did not want everyone staring at me so early in the morning, especially not thinking I got things wrong — though nothing about this was right. I was just ten years old.

FUNERAL

The limo swerved up in front of our perfectly manicured lawn, its front tire scraping the drenched curb. It had never once crossed my mind that we wouldn't be taking the minivan. Once I climbed inside, I was instantly overwhelmed by the unnecessary amount of space. We were awfully dressed up for so early in the morning.

It was a school day. We should have been waiting at the bus stop. Instead, we were being chauffeured to our mother's funeral. The dim-gray leather interior matched the scene outside the tinted windows. The silence was deafening. I gazed out at the familiar streets and houses, intentionally avoiding eye contact with my traveling companions. I wondered who had taken my brother shopping. Who had helped him button his dress shirt and suit jacket? Who tied his tie and combed his hair? I wasn't used to considering him until I was practically tripping over him. I should have been the one helping him. Was he scared too? It doesn't seem like anybody paid much attention to boys whose mothers died.

Panicked by the unease, an irresistible urge came over me. I spotted the radio mounted on the ceiling, and I reached overhead and turned the dial to ON. A harsh sound blasted out of the speakers. I recognized the first note. With tears in his eyes, Daddy stared at me in disbelief. I instantly jammed the button to the OFF position and slid back on the cold fake leather and stared a needle-pricking stare out the stormy window.

When we finally arrived at the church, I took an inventory of the cars in the parking lot. I didn't want to see anyone I knew. I was embarrassed. I wasn't prepared to be the center of attention. I really wasn't prepared to admit that Mama had lost her nine-month battle with cancer. Not when she fought so hard. Publicly mourning her severely diminished the hope we had held onto for so long — that she would keep going.

Daddy handed me the red hymnal he brought from the house. Mama had asked us to bring it home from church, and she kept it by her bed. As I stepped out of the limo and onto the pavement, I lost my grip. The hymnal fell to the cement. Little pieces of white paper fluttered in the air, eventually sticking to the wet pavement. I peeled off the scraps of paper. We all recognized the handwriting.

I pushed my way into the little circle of curious family members who had accumulated, and I discovered that these were Mama's funeral plans. I was angry at Daddy for allowing everyone to look at them. They could have been my secret. They were so personal. They were surely for me. Mama surely left them for me. The notes detailed her desire to be buried in a yellow pantsuit, which I remembered was purposefully hanging in a plastic dry-cleaning wrap in her closet. Clearly, not the lavender pantsuit someone had chosen. She listed the hymns to be played, none of which matched the cliché songs chosen by the pastor. So far, we were 0 for 2. Nothing about this was right. I fumbled with the tiny velvet button on my blouse, pretending to be distraught that it was getting wet even though the raindrops were beading right off the velvet. Meanwhile, the rain steadily slapped the pages of the hymnal left lying in the parking lot.

I had never been to a funeral before. One time we drove up to the town where Mama grew up because someone she knew had passed away. Mama and Daddy took turns waiting with us kids in the car while the other went inside. Clearly, Mama didn't want us to know what was going on inside. I wished I could stay inside the limo this time.

Inside the church, we were called to stand in the pulpit. Nobody told me that we had to go up there. Why would they put a girl who lost her Mama on display like that? Did they know the contortions I was going through just to hold back tears? I had been in the pulpit once before when I volunteered to be the acolyte who lit the candles before and after the Sunday service. I did not like the attention even then. I prayed to God over and over that I would not have to say something. Nobody had told me to think of something to say. This was humiliating.

Daddy's eyes were so puffy and sad. He stood at the podium in between my brother and me. This was the first time I had ever seen him address an audience. He began to read a poem he had personally written. I cringed in horror. I wanted to listen without feeling. I didn't want to feel the sweet words he was saying as he mourned Mama. I needed him to be strong. I could feel pity radiating from the pews. As our time in the spotlight was nearing its end, it occurred to me that everyone watching must have thought it unfathomable that I had not yet cried at my Mama's funeral. It had not even occurred to *me* that I might not cry. I certainly didn't want to meditate on what people would think of me if I didn't. What kind of daughter doesn't cry at their own mother's funeral? Did Mama want me to be crying right now? Would she be devastated? Would she think I did not love her?

Once Daddy finished speaking, the pastor ushered us into the very front pew. I had avoided eye contact with anyone in the audience, so I was disheartened to realize that my friends were sitting in the same row. They were fumbling with hymnals, making too much noise. I saw one friend smile. I was angry. They would go home to their Moms. They had no idea the things I had seen over the past nine months. They had no idea how hallowed these last moments of Mama being above ground were to me. They were so naïve, and I hated them for it.

After another strange procession, which we led in the limo, we arrived at the cemetery. It was the first time I had ever been to the place I would come to know so well. On the hill, there were three evergreen, velvet-covered chairs. The three of us walked toward the reserved thrones. Tufts of brown grass protruded from the icy dirt. Trails of people and cars boasting little magnetic flags lined the narrow paths as far as I could see. The people were standing under clouds of black umbrellas, their pity burning a hole in my back.

The pastor spoke about Mama in prayer, and tears lined my eyelids. I felt so exposed. I felt like she was so close. Suddenly, I decided that I would not cry. I had made it this far sans tears, and I promised myself that if I could just hold off another few hours, I would be in the comfort of my own bedroom where I could cry my eyes out in peace as I relived the day's events. I was not going to lose it now. Little moist droplets pooled right up to the rim of my eye. Had I tilted my head in the slightest, they surely would have spilled over. It became my purpose, my mission, not to cry. I pulled my mind's curtain down, and I forced myself to think of the bottle of purple nail polish, the one I had spilled on the white carpet, in hopes that it would somehow subdue the tears gripping my chest and throat. I meditated on the black wand. It made me neither happy nor sad. It was the only thing that worked.

Earlier, back at the church, I had stood in front the same casket that was soon going to be lowered into this huge dirt hole. That much I knew. I had seen funerals on TV. The finality of it all was setting in. There was nothing I would be able to do to slow time, to stop the chain of events that had already been set in motion. It just didn't seem like enough time had gone by, yet it felt like an eternity had passed. Nine months ago we were a normal, healthy family. I studied the creamy, silk-lined casket and looked at my Mama's pasty face for the last time, completely unaware of the straight strands of blonde hair on the back of my head I had been unable to reach by myself with the curling iron. Daddy had reached his hands into the casket to touch Mama's face. I felt paralyzed looking down at her. At the hospital, I had kissed the cold, clammy skin of my mother. With tears streaming down his face, Daddy readjusted the mass of yellow roses resting above her. He just kept touching things. All I wanted to do was beat up whoever made her look this way and throw them into the six-foot hole we were now standing in front of. She would be buried in her wig.

I had already lived three days motherless. Three days were still short enough to feel temporary. I had taken a mental snapshot of her face and her body at the church, knowing that it would be the last time I ever saw my Mama's sweet face. She was the first face I ever laid eyes on when I came into this world, and now this would be the last time I ever saw her. I never wanted to forget her.

The casket was slowly lowered into the icy earth by a pulley system. Everything was happening too quickly. While everyone's head was bowed in prayer, I cautiously lifted my gaze. A single teardrop slipped to my rouged cheek. It was the only tear I shed all day.

Amanda M. Harding

The Woman of the House

Part Two

WHAT WE LOST

The Woman of the House

MAMA

My mother was everything you would dream of a mother to be. She was a smalltown girl from Beavertown, Pennsylvania. She was kind, sweet, and smart. After high school she was a foreign exchange student in Brazil where she learned to speak Portuguese. I've always wondered what inspired a smalltown girl to move to Brazil. My Mama made friends everywhere she went and easily chatted amongst the other mothers at school functions. She took my brother and me on special shopping trips when we behaved, to the pool in the summer, and set up playdates with our friends at our house. Though I'm sure she didn't love our green minivan, she chauffeured us around happily. She constantly told me to clean my room and would often do it for me without complaining. Every Christmas we took a family vacation to Fort Myers Beach, Florida, and our summer vacations were at Rehoboth Beach, Delaware, and boating and camping at Raystown Lake, Pennsylvania. Mama threw us lavish birthday parties and always gave the perfect gifts.

I don't remember Mama's favorite meals to cook, but she was always trying recipes out of one of her new diet cookbooks. I was very stubborn and strong-willed as a child. Yet somehow she always managed to be patient with me, always enthusiastic to teach me life lessons. At Girl Scout camp, she was in charge of a group of junior-high school girls and I remember seeing her for the first time easily talking to the older girls about whatever it was that older girls talked about. They liked her. I stored that memory in the back of my mind, thinking one day I would want to tell her things like that and laugh with her in that older sort of way. One day we could be really good friends.

Mama had a huge crush on George Clooney and subsequently never missed an episode of ER. As long as I can remember, Mama always kept her hair short and colored. She always took me to the salon with her as a girls' day out. When Mama was a little girl my grandma made her keep a pixie cut which she despised, and so, Mama was always proud of my long blond hair.

I know she wanted the best for my brother and me. I know that we made her a some sort of special kind of happy even when we were terribly difficult to handle. She was always worried about us and very conscientious of what we were doing and how we were feeling. Mama was known for not following through with her threats of punishment, so it was very easy to win her over. She always cut the dark spot out of the banana before carefully slicing each piece and placing in our bowl of Rice Krispies. She kissed us goodnight every night and taught me how to say bedtime prayers. She insisted that we say grace at family dinners. She had a funny sense of humor that I never got to know as an adult.

When she would catch me and my best friend watching Singled Out on MTV after school, she would get angry, but she tried her best not to embarrass me in front of my friends. She encouraged me to do dance, softball, basketball, theater, and crafts, basically whatever interested me. She made sure we grew up in a safe upper-middle-class neighborhood and that we had perfectly themed and coordinated bedrooms. She loved that I played the flute and encouraged me to practice. She took pride in her coordinating Pfaltzgraff dinnerware set and enjoyed serving the family meals on them. She hand-sewed our Halloween costumes. She was my childhood. She loved to read and was an amazing speller. She never missed a detail. She stopped working at the family business when we were in elementary school. I doubt my grandparents were very supportive of this, as my Daddy was left to work long hours in order to support our lifestyle, but I am sure thankful for every extra second I was able to spend with my Mama.

The Woman of the House

Part Three

GRIEF IS

The Woman of the House

GRIEF IS

Grief for me was learning how to accept my new membership into this motherless-daughter society and all of the new roles associated with it. I've had many adults, who watched me grow up, marvel at my ability to cope with Mama's death. If coping equaled surviving, then, yes, I was coping pretty well on the outside.

Grief has many facets. It's not predictable. Rather, it's cyclical and erratic. In the beginning, you are in survival mode, and then once things have slowed down, the real grieving sets in. It's not until after the funeral when you walk into your house that you realize what you've actually lost. Suppressed emotions, that you may or may not even know you held, will begin to bubble to the surface, begging to be dealt with. As an adolescent, sometimes I was capable of properly dealing with such emotions; sometimes I was not. Regardless, the emotions will keep coming until they are processed and relieved.

My grief is triggered by the following situations: holidays, anniversaries, finding her belongings in junk drawers, her handwriting in the address book, her car in the garage, Daddy crying in church, mail addressed to her, telemarketers asking to speak to her, Your Mama jokes, cemeteries, filling out forms, the thought of losing someone else, and knowing that new people in my life will never get to know her and what she was like. Grief can also rear its head at the most unexpected things such as a simple smell or memory.

With time, grief can easily be identified and categorized into stages of intensity. Grief, I've learned, is not a bad thing at all. It's replaying the same events but walking away with different conclusions each time. It's a process. It's a lifetime membership.

SOCKS

In junior high, toe socks were the fad. Everyone had these socks that were brightly striped and had a separate slot for each toe. We used to pull the brightly colored socks up to our knees and then show them off by wearing flip-flops. One of my more popular friends had three older sisters, and hence, she was always at the forefront of the newest trends. One day at track practice she wore a pair of the fuzziest, softest pink socks I had ever seen.

Everyone admired them, and I was already planning on how I was going to get them that weekend.

A few nights later my Nan was visiting my Mama in her hospital room when we walked in. I saw rumpled tissue paper peeking out of a Hecht's box on the nightstand. Mama was lying in her hospital bed. It was adjusted to the shape of a V so that she could sit up to talk. She didn't move her hands much anymore because they were so bruised and tangled in IVs. I was wearing my dance leotard, the one she had helped me pick out. I had the white skirt wrapped around my ever-evolving hips. I was the tallest girl in my dance class, and I felt peculiar. I sat down in the chair next to the nightstand, and I lifted the box to see what Nan had brought her. Inside the box were long fuzzy white socks with little rubber pads on the bottom. They had gold stitching across the toes. I wanted those socks so badly. I wanted to wear them to school under my jeans. Everyone would love them. It crossed my mind that Mama would have let me have them if I asked her. However, I couldn't bring myself to be so selfish. She deserved them. She needed them.

A few days later Daddy brought us to the hospital again. The nurses had moved Mama into a larger room. It was brand new. There was furniture to make it seem like you were not in a hospital. The walls were a fresh yellow, and the trim was a grass-green color. The furniture was modern and clean. We hadn't been allowed to see her for two days. The new room had several teak doors with skinny glass windows in them so the nurses could be in the room while not intruding on the patient. Mama was lying in bed. I sat on the new chair in front of her bed beneath the TV mounted overhead. There was a sitcom playing softly in the background. Mama was silent. A plastic tube was wrapped around her ears and under her nose. I could see the plastic bag under the comforter filling with a dark brown liquid. Sometimes the nurses would come in to change it, and we would leave the room to give Mama privacy. Daddy was in a good mood when we got there that day. He sat by Mama's side and touched her face. He believed in miracles.

A thin, young man with a long white coat came in the room. He was holding his clipboard tight to his chest. Though he had already entered, he tapped lightly on the door for good measure. We all looked up at him. He hovered near the door. He looked at me and then at my brother, saying hello to nobody in particular. He asked Daddy if he could speak with him in the separate room. I saw them through the mesh wire in the skinny glass window. Daddy's face turned red. He looked like he had seen a ghost. He was so naïve that day walking in there with us. Asking us, in a childlike voice, "Doesn't Mama look good today?" Saying, "Hi, sweetheart." Kissing her forehead.

The doctor took that from him. Daddy stood there alone. The doctor stopped talking, but Daddy just stared. His posture slumped. Hi shoulders caved in. I saw him convulse. He just looked helpless. The veins in his eyes turned red. He looked so confused. He turned around and looked at me through the skinny glass window. I had wanted to warn Daddy that I knew Mama was going to die. I wanted to tell him months ago. I was so sorry.

Daddy took the tissue the doctor had set on the counter top and walked back in to our room. His face was pale. Tears were streaming down his stubbled face. It was only Mama, Daddy, my brother and me in the room now. Daddy was wearing a shirt Mama had bought him a few years ago. Daddy took us outside into the hallway and told us that Mama was going to die.

We sat in silence all day, save the times we told her we loved her. Daddy kept telling us to go give her a kiss and tell her we loved her. Like we could save her. He held a little Styrofoam cup in his hand. There was a straw with a green cube sponge. He would dip it in the cup and press it to Mama's cracked lips. Mama never responded. In Sunday school, we had watched a movie about Jesus on the cross. I specifically remember them showing men in robes wrapping cloth around gigantic pieces of wood until it resembled a large Q-Tip. Then the robed men soaked the cloth in vinegar and held it up to Jesus' mouth while he bled to death on the cross. I knew the Styrofoam cup wasn't full of vinegar, but I felt something for the first time witnessing Mama's suffering and Daddy's desperate attempt to comfort her.

It was heartbreaking witnessing this human act of kindness. As the afternoon turned into evening, my mind became blurry. Did I want to get this over with? Daddy led us to a waiting room on the far end of the hallway where there were orange vinyl lounge chairs and coloring books. We were the only children on the floor. We were always the only children in that wing of the hospital. The window faced the mountains and the river and the bridge. The steel beams of the bridge were illuminated by Christmas lights. It was comforting, those lights. They reminded me of home. And though the sunset was vibrantly orange, the ice in the river, and the cool blue wisps of color in the sky made everything feel chilly.

Our counselor came in and handed us crayons and paper. I held a crayon in my hand wanting to make a masterpiece so I could keep it with me later and say this was from the day Mama died. It would be famous; it would be passionate. Instead, when I put the bulky crayon to the plain small paper, my work was ugly and childish. The waxy crayon could not convey the intricacies of my feelings. I gazed out the window feeling wise beyond my years. I hadn't talked to my friends. I hadn't been to school in days.

I recognized the voices of relatives echoing from down the hall. Peeking out the door, I saw Grandma had arrived with my aunts. She lived two hours away. She had her little black pocketbook in her hand, and she did not look scared. She did not talk to us. I knew she wished she could have had her daughter to herself in private. But wishes did not always come true.

When we walked in the room, everyone looked down at the floor. My aunts hugged us. Daddy was sitting in the corner next to Mama's bed crying. Mama's eyes were randomly opening and closing. She was tugging at the plastic tubes on her face and moving her hands violently like she was trapped. But she wasn't. When we came close, she stopped. She pulled her bruised and bony hand up to her face and gently unwrapped the tubes from behind her ears. The tube slid off to the side of her pillow. Her wedding ring was far too loose on her finger. Her skin was pasty and clammy. She gestured for me to come by her with a look I was certain was a smile. Daddy told me it was okay. I didn't want to hurt her. I lay down next to her while everyone watched. Her gown was falling off of her shoulders. I told her I loved her. She was still. My poor little brother. He came up next to me and held my hand and watched her. He loved my Mama so much. He was so scared.

A few female nurses came in and tried to readjust the tubes on Mama's ears, yet she kept moaning and turning her head in protest as they came near her. Then noises started blaring. We were ushered out of the room in to the hallway while everyone else slowly entered, bundled in their jackets and talking in hushed voices. I heard a loud cry.

Shortly after, Daddy came in to the waiting room, held up by our pastor. The three of us sat on the orange vinyl couch and prayed as Mama's spirit was being lifted onto the back of an angel and carried above the ceiling, out of the hospital, above the sky, and into Heaven to be with God. When it was done, we were ushered out of the room to go on with our lives. We would never have to come back again. As we walked past Mama's room, the only thing I saw through the glass window was the golden fabric of her socks peeking out from under a white cloth.

HAMSTERS

We were not allowed to have pets when we were growing up. Mama and Daddy said we weren't responsible enough. One year, however, Mama finally announced that we were allowed to get hamsters. I imagine this decision had something to do with the incessant, and possibly intolerable, whining and begging we had subjected Mama to. Mama drove us to the pet shop down the street, and she let me pick out a brown and white female that I named Brownie. My brother picked out an all-white male and named him Nutty. We were fascinated by them. At first, we were too scared to actually pick them up, afraid of their sharp teeth. Soon, however, we were carrying them around in our pockets and teaching them how to climb the steps. Brownie even had several litters of baby hamsters. We adored those little critters.

Well, one morning I came downstairs and Mama looked worried. I walked over to the cage like I did every morning to give Brownie a treat when I noticed that she was not moving. I poked at her through the metal bars, and she was still. Mama put her arm around me with tears in her eyes. I started bawling. We were supposed to go on a field trip that day, and if I was late I would miss the bus. Mama told me I didn't have to go, that she would call my teacher and let her know what happened. I saw the look of sadness in Mama's eyes as she watched us experience grief for the first time. I imagine as much as she wanted to always be able to protect us from things like that, and up to this point had always been able to, she saw the significance of this moment.

CHRISTMAS

The first Christmas after cancer, Daddy bought us the largest Christmas tree he could find. I had decorated the house exactly the way Mama had the year before, except I did not hang her stocking on the fireplace. Under the tree were awkwardly wrapped TV sets. Most of Santa's name tags were in Nan's handwriting, but some of them were in Daddy's too. Mama used to buy me a Lennox Christmas ornament every year. I had ten ornaments. I would never get another one. I thought about purchasing the rest of the collection on eBay, but the very thought made me sad. That's not the way it was supposed to be.

That same year I kept up Mama's tradition of sending Christmas cards to everyone in our address book. I wanted people to think that we were still normal, like we hadn't missed a beat. I told, not asked, Daddy that I wanted to send the cards out like we did every year. Without asking any questions, he came home with several large packs of Christmas cards and stamps.

I created the list of recipients, and I carefully handwrote each name from Mama's address book on to the front of the envelopes. I had Daddy and my brother sign their names. I've done this every year since we lost Mama.

MAMA'S DEATH

The anniversary of Mama's death marked a new holiday on our family calendar. A new date to remember. A previously unimportant date that now held significant meaning. The first year after cancer, Daddy took my brother and me to Mama's favorite restaurant, the Progress Grille, for dinner. Whenever Mama and Daddy went there for dinner, which was very rarely, Mama would bring me home a leftover crab cake. They were her favorite. We didn't talk about Mama or the reason for the occasion at all during this dinner. A year had passed. We were still grieving in our own distorted ways. After dinner Daddy drove us to the cemetery and we stood silently at her grave while Daddy cleaned the marble edges with a rag and placed a bouquet of flowers on the stone. In the moonlight, I could see the exhaust from the minivan and hear the soft hum of the engine.

EASTER

On Easter, our church always held a sunrise service in the same cemetery that Mama was buried in. It was still very chilly in those mornings. I didn't have an appropriate Easter dress to wear, so I woke up when it was still dark and tiptoed into Mama's closet to try to find something to wear. I wanted to look pretty. While Daddy was getting ready, I went into the closet and took Mama's Etienne Aigner sandals. The grass at the cemetery was cool and damp with dew. Little blades of grass stuck to my white sandals. I worried that Mama's friends at church would recognize her shoes and think it was odd. Daddy never said anything.

Daddy stood between us and put his hands on our backs as we walked up the narrow path to the part of the cemetery where the white stone statues were displayed to join the rest of the congregation. The orange sun was hovering below the horizon, ready for its glorious approach upwards. Usually about fifty people attended the sunrise service. We stood and sang lovely hymns a cappella that echoed throughout the cemetery. I could feel the angels all around. The message was always the same, but I found a renewed peace in it. As we spoke of Jesus' tomb being empty at sunrise, the sun would rise beyond the preacher. The cold air cleansed my lungs, and the smell of fresh colognes and perfumes in the morning air made me feel so alive, so invigorated. When the service concluded, and the sun had risen, it brought with it the promise of Mama's presence in our daily lives.

After the service, we took the long walk down the hill to Mama's grave. We put yellow tulips in a purple foiled pot on her grave while the congregation trickled past us, knowingly. After the invigorating service, I was able to clearly reflect on how far we had come since that solemn day when Mama was laid to rest below our very feet.

HIGH SCHOOL GRADUATION

As a high school graduation gift, my grandma and aunt made my brother and me each a scrapbook with black and white pictures of our grandparents and Mama when she was a little girl. They wrote detailed captions below each picture, which let me in on a whole new world that I never knew existed. They also had made quilts for each of us out of sections of Mama's old dresses and favorite T-shirts.

I tried so hard to hold back the tears when I was presented with this gift. I wanted so badly to tell them it was the greatest gift I had ever received in my entire life. I thanked them multiple times. I was so caught off guard by their generosity and thoughtfulness at the time that it was difficult for me to show them how much this gift meant to me. I know tears would have said more than words, but I did not allow myself to break down. I could not wait to take the scrapbook home and look at it. Each time my aunt tried to describe one of the black-and-white pictures to me I could barely make a sound, I was so choked up. But this scrapbook connected so many constellations that would have otherwise been nameless in the galaxy of all the things I didn't know about my Mama.

The Woman of the House

Part Four

EVERY LOSS IS UNIQUE

The Woman of the House

EVERY LOSS IS UNIQUE

I've sometimes wondered if death by terminal illness is more of a blessing or a curse than death by a random act. In a way, her terminal cancer gave us the opportunity to sort of get a head start on the grieving process. It became a defining moment in each of our lives. Acknowledging its inevitability reminded us that we could ensure closure. We could tell her how much we loved her more often than we would have otherwise. We could choose our words, our actions, the memories we would remember her by.

At the same time, Mama had the opportunity to prepare things for us in her inevitable absence. This is where I find the greatest blessing, and I am thankful to God for giving her the ability and foresight to do so even when she was literally dying and in pain.

SOMETHING

I always dreamed that Mama left behind something for me. I always held out hope that she did and it was my job to find it. I used to scour the house for hours, always ending up sitting on top of a pile of her clothes on the floor of her walk-in closet. I was looking for clues to her past that I might have overlooked when I was too young to notice. I found letters and notes and to-do lists. I only ever went in her closet when the house was empty.

One time I found a love letter written in Portuguese. It was from a man she was obviously dating when she was a foreign exchange student in Brazil. I spent hours in the library with a Portuguese dictionary figuring this out. It was me who, ten years after her death, cleaned out her makeup and nail polish shoebox and threw them out. It was me who took her clothing that was still hanging in the closet where she left it and put the clothes in the car and dropped them off at Goodwill. Daddy couldn't bear to do it. We never talked about it, the timing was right. I did not need those things to know her.

I was certain that if Mama had taken the time to plan out the details of her own funeral, then surely she must have left something behind for me too. And, sure enough, a few years later, I was organizing the old VHS Tapes in her closet, which had now begun to resemble a multi-purpose storage room, when I found several unlabeled cassette tapes.

I took them into my bedroom and rummaged through my nightstand until I pulled out my old Walkman tape player. I played the tapes, with the old foam headphones on my ears. Mama's voice came out of the little padded speaker. I laid back onto my pink bedspread and held on to my teddy bear for dear life as I listened to her voice. My children would be able to listen to their grandma one day.

She recorded the tape herself while she was lying in my brother's bed on a Sunday morning. We went to church that morning without her because the perfumes in the church made her nauseous. I heard her pause and begin to cry when she said she was sure I was doing wonderfully as the acolyte that morning; she wished she could have been there.

I always imagined that if there was ever a fire in our house, the very first thing I would do was collect every tape and family picture of her and throw them out of the house to safety. They are the only proof left that I once was normal and had a normal family and a mother. Throughout the years, we have discovered more tapes, and I always hold out hope that there will be more. Just one more, I pray.

THE LETTER

Daddy was pouring instant mashed potatoes into a pot on the stove when the phone rang. I was still in my sweaty field hockey uniform. My brother was attempting to do his math homework at the counter. Daddy picked up the phone, nodded, and then set the phone down and walked into the other room. He yelled to me to hang up the phone in the kitchen. I had developed a bad habit of eavesdropping, and I had become skilled at it. So, without putting the phone down, I clicked the bar on the receiver so it would sound like I hung up and then I covered the phone with my palm and motioned to my brother to be quiet. I heard our babysitter tell Daddy that she had found a letter on the computer that Mama started writing to us. It was quite a few pages; unfinished for obvious reasons. When I was certain their conversation was wrapping up, I gently held the bar down with my finger and slid the phone back onto the receiver. Daddy returned to the kitchen as though nothing had happened. I smelled burning potato flakes. With tears in his voice, Daddy told us that our babysitter had found a letter from Mama that we could read one day.

Every morning, for eight years, I longed to find a neatly stacked pile of paper sitting on the kitchen table next to my Cheerios. For some reason unbeknownst to me, Daddy never showed me the letter, even though he sporadically referenced its existence. I was squirming to find it and reveal its agonizing secrets. When would Daddy think I was ready to read it? As the years passed, I worried that Mama's letter could never live up to my ever expanding expectations.

One summer day, I was at the house alone. I was snooping through closets for things I might want to bring to college with me. In the downstairs hallway closet, I spotted a stack of newspaper articles. Mostly sports articles about my brother and me. I thought I had seen them all before. However, I stood on a kitchen chair and wiggled the sheets out from under a heavy candelabrum. I soon became conscious of what I was holding.

After all these years of curiosity, I had found Mama's letter. I slid the chair on the hardwood floor exactly in its original place. Then I raced up the carpeted steps to my bedroom. Sitting Indian-style on the floor of my walk-in closet with the door shut, I started reading. My heart was pounding in my ears. Thudding. Adrenaline was swirling and gushing through my veins. Yet, I heard her voice clearly. Drops of tears swelled from my eyelids. I couldn't take my eyes off the page. Tears plopped and spattered onto the paper. I flipped each page carefully, wishing they would go on forever. It was twelve pages in total.

The letter was actually a memoir printed on white computer paper. I wondered how Mama had intended us to find it. The original draft had been created on our desktop computer, so I assumed our babysitter had printed it for Daddy since he wasn't exactly adept when it came to the computer. Regardless, the content and the fact that it existed at all was glorious. The fact that Mama had taken the time to prepare something so honest and sweet and powerful reminded me of how much I missed her. Her story was that of a woman, a sister, a wife, a mother, a lover, a child, a teacher, a girl. I had no idea my Mama was capable of this. This was a gift that she didn't have to give us. Though, I imagine the pleasure was hers to write even more so than for us to read.

I didn't think I would ever be able to fully catalog the joy I felt holding this manual, if you will, in my hands. Mama detailed secret things I suspected she knew only a daughter would want to take away. She didn't hold back anything. She gave us words of advice and her personal experiences to back it up. Her intentions weren't for us to have to go through life without her. She used her talent of writing to answer questions she knew we would have later in life that she wouldn't be there to answer. She specifically gave me a lot of advice. Advice only a mother could give her daughter. She knew the role I was going to have to fill, and she wanted to prepare me the best she could. That was so Mama. She knew I would be cheated of this luxury my whole life.

There was no cancer in her words. She was not bald. She had a brilliantly rich story to tell. The story I will tell my children. The story of a life lived wonderfully and the particular lessons and memories she cherished. I don't know if she edited the letter. I wonder. I thought back to the days when

I came home from school and she was in the computer room. How selfless of her. Her letter is the most precious thing I've ever owned. A manual I could refer to when I needed to hear her voice. I used to think how proud Mama would be if she could see how Daddy raised us. But now I know that Mama knew. She had always known.

I was crying all the unshed tears I had bottled up inside of me. This was an answered prayer. I put the letter in my Jansport backpack and rode my bike to the supermarket where I made five photocopies of it. I am reminded of the phrase, "I didn't have time to write you a note so I wrote you a book." She put only what she thought we needed to know in these twelve pages. How precious. I savored every sentence. This kind of thirst could never be sated. I placed the original back where I had accidentally found it. Every time I read one of my photocopied versions, I felt my Mama's unconditional love radiating from the pages. A mother's love transcends all emotions, and this little memento serves as a tangible reminder that I have personally known the love a mother who loved her family more than anything else in this world.

The detail lover in me is highly aware that the first sentence in a paragraph sets the tone for the rest of the narrative. It was the answer to a question I hadn't known I was asking in my own life. Mama's letter, titled Small Town Girl, began, "I have always wanted to write a novel." I would write a book.

The Woman of the House

Part Five

FEELING DIFFERENT

The Woman of the House

FEELING DIFFERENT

I never considered myself as coming from a single-parent home. I had friends who were raised by single moms as the result of a divorce, but I did not know anyone who was raised by a single father. Especially a widowed single father. Our situation was unique in our community at the time. Unique was not something I was going for as a pre-teen who just wanted to fit in, if not fly under the radar altogether.

In junior high and high school, I felt older and wiser than all my friends. As a result, I preferred to make friends with kids who were older than me. I liked older boys. I lost my ability to be silly and innocent, not because I didn't want to be (I wanted nothing more), but because I had seen too much. I had come back to school with a new outlook on life, a big-picture outlook. I teetered on the thin line of taking the wrong path often, but I was always able to recover and steer clear.

I was the only teenager I knew who worried about her brother and father constantly. I worried about being responsible for keeping the household together in the emotional sense. I was aware that none of my friends could relate to me and what I was going through, and so I rarely talked about my feelings. It wasn't their fault.

It wasn't until college, when I moved to a brand new city a thousand miles from home that I was able to share my story with my new friends. At nineteen and twenty, my new friends were more emotionally mature and old enough to have experienced hardships of their own — I felt like everyone my age had finally caught up to me. We all came from different backgrounds, and our stories were the glue that bonded us together.

Still today, at twenty-five years old, I feel like women who have mothers "have the key" to womanhood that I do not. I still struggle with feminine things like going to birthday parties and bridal showers. I wonder if I am wearing the right outfit. I agonize over whether or not I bought the right type of gift and wrapped it as nicely as the other gifts.

SOCIAL ANXIETY

In high school, instead of going to Barnes & Noble for a coffee and to look at the latest chick-lit bestseller, I was secretly browsing the self-help aisles. I knew something was off. I was different, after all. A crucial and tangible part of me was missing, and I didn't know what to do about it. I needed to somehow define my symptoms and find others who had overcome them. I hoped I could find a cure in these books. The emergence of the Internet also gave me hope. I certainly couldn't talk to Daddy about this. And I was already long done with counseling. I had turned down Daddy's attempts to join a support group with children my age because I knew I would be too embarrassed to open up. Thus, I tried to deal with my confusing emotions and behaviors in the privacy of my own adolescent mind.

Based on my "research," I diagnosed myself with social anxiety. It was the strangest thing. Before cancer, I was quite outgoing, and relationships and friendships came easily to me. Externally, I was actually thriving, but internally I was struggling with how to act in all social situations.

I longed for the confident, secure girl that I once was. I wanted to be able to carelessly laugh and play with my friends, but either I was different to them or they were different to me now. Either way, I was different. I didn't laugh at the things they found funny. I didn't find anything funny anymore. At the same time, I was more desperate than ever for everyone's approval. My Daddy probably noticed this, unbeknownst to me, and so he made sure to uphold Mama's tradition of throwing us lavish birthday parties at arcades and hotels and would surprise us with spontaneous trips in limos. I love Daddy for this, and I could see the joy our joy brought him.

The sad part is that in these moments I would let myself go and be having such a good time but then suddenly I would remember that Mama wasn't there to bring out the cake and sing to me. This realization would snap me back to feeling sad despite all the happiness I was enjoying and Daddy's efforts to make me happy. At one birthday party, I actually started crying during the night, and all my friends heard. I just wanted to be alone, but I didn't know why.

I played softball, basketball, and field hockey year-round. I was on three different teams for each sport. My brother had a similar schedule. Daddy never missed a game or complained about our involvement. I am very grateful for this. The practices and games kept me busy and involved with others, which is definitely a good thing. In a way, I was too busy to be depressed. I was also fortunate that my coaches were very caring and attentive.

A basketball coach once told me that I was tenacious. I asked Daddy what that meant. He told me that it meant that I was persistent and that this was a compliment. Another coach once told me that he felt like "I was on a mission." These comments are special to me. My coaches saw past the broken girl to the fire in my heart — the fire that was there before cancer. Mama and Daddy had instilled in me a sense of self-worth, and it was neat to hear confirmation from people I highly respected of what I was beginning to believe in myself. They thought I would be okay. In fact, it was possible that I might even turn out better than okay. It would be up to me to ignite whatever spark was left.

SIBLINGS

Another duty to take on as the woman of the house was the well-being of my younger brother. Only seven years old at the time of my Mama's death, my brother was a very important third of our family. Nan told me that when Mama was dying, she would lie with him and snuggle with him in his bed. He was a Mama's boy if there ever was one. I was much more like my Daddy even though I spent more time with Mama. My brother was gentle, sweet, and needy in the most innocent little-boy way. I knew instantly that he was going to need to be cared for and protected, but I was also his older sister, and we were entering that stage where we weren't supposed to get along. Though we fought often, out of obligatory social norms, we had a special bond. He clung to me; I was the woman of the house, the closest thing to his Mama.

I was being specially treated and protected by my grandmas, aunts, and family friends. A girl losing her mother is surely tragic, and she needs to be especially cared for. Yet I always had an underlying concern for my little brother because, as far as I was aware, he was not receiving the same special treatment. I guess they thought he could tough it out. I worried that he had no one to talk to. Knowing what I knew about the sweet relationship he and my Mama shared, I made it a point to look out for him. Over the years that meant buying him special things from the grocery store, watching his baseball games, tattling on him to keep him out of trouble, and preaching to him whenever necessary. He had a healthy level of respect for me that enabled me to get away with this type of mothering. I cared deeply for my hurting little brother. I worry every day about the hurt he holds inside. I've encouraged him to seek counseling throughout the years, and once I was more comfortable talking about Mama out loud, I urged myself to tell him things about her. I figured this probably delighted him the same way I was delighted to hear new things about her.

Amanda M. Harding

The Woman of the House

Amanda M. Harding

Part Six

CHANGES AT HOME

The Woman of the House

CHANGES AT HOME

Living with a mother who had a terminal illness was heartbreaking. We witnessed Mama's body being overtaken by tumors I never saw. She could no longer do all of the things around the house that she used to do. Sadly, I still expected her to and was disappointed when I noticed the changes. Even the way she talked to me sort of changed. I think she wanted to keep me her innocent little girl for as long as she could. She knew after she was gone that would be taken away from me. So she went out of her way to make our days special.

I was always closest to my Mama even though I was more like my Daddy. We were used to the way she ran the household. There were so many things that we took for granted and did not thank her for. So many things just got done and went unnoticed until we had to do them ourselves. After she passed away, I was especially frustrated with the new ways things were getting done — and not getting done. It took years to establish a routine and

⌐ housekeeper who cleaned once a month. Daddy was actually a neat freak, which didn't always fit with my idea of a comforting, lived-in home.

When something worked, we stuck with it. If it didn't, we usually argued and then figured it out. These moments helped us bond as a new family unit. It was difficult to see Daddy frustrated, and in the first three or four years after Mama died, he was often frustrated. He took out his anger on us in peculiar ways, such as throwing my clothes out the front door once when I refused to clean my room. It was just odd. I remembered learning in counseling not to take these sorts of things personally, and so I didn't. I knew dealing with teenagers wasn't easy.

I did worry about Daddy dating. I would not tolerate a new woman in our house. It would have been too much to handle early on. When we were in high school, Daddy did start going out for a drink after we were in bed and he had packed our lunches. When he finally brought a date to meet us, I was very friendly, secretly hoping I would like her. None of his dating amounted to anything, as far as I was concerned. He did not date anyone seriously until I moved away to college. I have to say I think that was for the best. I don't think I could have handled a new woman in the picture, but maybe if she was the right one, I could have. I didn't necessarily see his dating as betraying my Mom. I was genuinely more concerned with my ability to cope with a new role in the house again.

I sometimes worried that when my brother left for college, Daddy would struggle with an empty nest. At the same time, I also thought it was exactly what he needed. I recognized that Daddy needed somebody besides us. The ultimate goal of raising children is to send them out into the world to start their own families. Daddy had done an excellent job of raising us to be mature, self-sufficient, responsible adults. He had devoted his entire life to fulfilling Mama's request.

COOKING

I do not remember much about my grandparents before cancer. They were very well off, and my Nan dressed lavishly in whites, creams, and gold. A lot of gold. Gold necklaces cloaked her neckline, and gold bracelets adorned her wrists. She drove a lovely royal blue Mercedes. Pap drove a work van. All of their telephones smelled of Pap's Phillies cigars, and his blue pinstriped work shirts were dotted with tiny burn marks.

I remember their new house had white carpet in the kitchen. Mama just couldn't get over that. I overheard Mama telling someone that my Nan did not appreciate that we touched everything in her house. There was some distance.

We were family, nonetheless. I often remind my husband that if all families and in-laws were perfect and desired, there would not exist as many movies and punch lines. Nan took me and my older cousin to their condo in Marco Island, Florida, every summer since I can remember. It was my favorite vacation of the year, always during summer break. Mama and Daddy would give me a $100 bill to securely hide in my jean over-the-shoulder purse. Mama would make sure all my clothes were pressed and neatly packed before I left.

It was important to Nan that our hair was in ribbons and our clothes perfectly matching. She loved to buy us expensive clothing for Christmas and holidays. I got a lot of hand-me-downs from my older cousin.

After cancer, however, I saw my grandparents in a new light. Having a family business enabled my grandparents to help out in ways that actually saved our family. Nan and my aunts would take me shopping and give us rides when Mama and Daddy were at hospital appointments. We spent many nights at Nan's house so that Daddy could continue to put in his long hours. I felt at home at Nan's house — even if she did cover our chairs with towels. She is such a loving mother and wife, and it was from her that I took lessons shortly after Mama passed away. I was not the sweet, feminine granddaughter she had set out to groom, but I had potential. Nan cooked us many, many meals before, during, and after cancer. Beef noodles, pork and sauerkraut, chicken and waffles, ham, green beans, and potato soup, shepherd's pie, butter noodles, spaghetti, and so forth. I find home in those meals. However, every few weeks she would complain that we had not returned her Tupperware. Where did we hide it?

MORPHINE

When I think of Mama at the hospital, it is of dusty white skin, wiry strands of peach fuzz sprouting on her scalp, and two protruding bones that are all that's left of where her eyebrows once grew. Her cheeks are flushed; she is smiling when she sees me. Beneath her patterned gown, her arms are a canvas of tape, gauze, needles, and plastic tubing. There's a plastic sack on the side of her bed that I once watched fill with a deep yellow urine. Through the openings in her gown, I can see her little legs, and it makes me uncomfortable. She always wanted to be thin. I remember doing crunches next to her on the floor as we watched the Abs of Steel video. Mama's chest is completely flat, and, though I've never seen the scars, I visualize the two thick, permanent reminders. Mama told me she would show me one day.

I learn what morphine is and hear it referenced often. She tries so hard to fight the sleep that the morphine causes when we are visiting her. She smiles and she tries so hard to stay awake for us. Each time we see her it takes us a few minutes to get comfortable. But Mama makes it easy for us because she hugs us and talks to us and asks us questions about our day. It seems so silly and childish to fight or complain in front of her and, yet, sometimes we do. Because we are scared and sad and we are children.

I am very aware that we are living a life separate from her. When it gets dark out, we go to the cafeteria for dinner and then we get to leave. We get to go; we are free. Oh, Mama. She must be terribly lonely all day, awaiting our arrival. Perhaps we are the best part of her day. She says we are. She tells us about the food she eats each day and the nurses and doctors that she sees and the friends who come to visit her. She somehow manages to have lively conversations that are not indicative of her awful illness. She is so graceful.

I sit in the hospital chairs, and I try to figure out the cure to cancer. I am sure that it is something very simple. Perhaps it's caused by watching too much TV or smoking or drinking. But Mama didn't smoke or drink. I don't have much confidence in these doctors. One time I read an article in a magazine about breastfeeding and breast cancer. I'm convinced that there is a link, but I don't know if Mama breastfed me or not. I wonder where I will be the day the cure for cancer is found.

ROOT BEER

After cancer, at ten years old, I was the main grocery shopper. Daddy pretty much gave me free rein to get what we needed for the house. I embraced the responsibility. One morning, I was pushing the cart down the soda aisle (we never were allowed to have soda in the house) when I spotted a glistening six-pack of root beer. I thought the bottles would be neat to drink out of when I had my friends over. I asked Daddy if I could get it and he agreed. So, I carefully picked up the carton and placed it in the cart. I saw Daddy staring at the label. He looked concerned and told me to get a different brand. I was curious and asked him why. He matter-of-factly told me that the brand IBC was the same acronym used for the type of cancer Mama had. Inflammatory Breast Cancer.

STRAWBERRIES

On bright and cheery summer mornings, Mama took us to the local strawberry farm. She made sure we were lathered in sunscreen before piling us into the minivan. We were allowed to pick as many blueberries or strawberries as we could fit into our little green plastic containers. She would let us snack on the fresh berries while we picked. At home Mama and I would make strawberry shortcake for dessert, and she would let me carefully slice the strawberries and cover them in a heavy dose of sugar. I will always remember the little ways in which she allowed us to be independent.

After cancer, I was in charge of planting the potted flowers each spring. Daddy would drive me to the flower nursery, and I would pick out as many different arrangements as I could budget with the money that he gave me. While we were in the car I would make a list of all the pots we had and how many of each type of flower we would need. Daddy never gave me any sort of direction on the matter, which pleased me. When I was finished shopping, I would find Daddy, and he would load the bags of dirt and containers of flowers into the car while I paid at the register. I would spend the afternoon in the front yard, covered in dirt, reminiscing on the arrangements Mama used to make. I loved planting the flowers, watering them, and seeing them bloom. Each time a pot bloomed, I was reminded of the miracle involved. We take for granted, far too often, that flowers bloom. I loved that Daddy trusted me with what used to be Mama's task.

Before cancer, Mama had planted roses underneath our wooden deck. They were a peachy pink color. They were absolutely lovely. Their fragrance was divine. Daddy tended to the roses like they were his special project. He pruned them in the winter and packed the little stubs with a homemade concoction of fertilizer in a makeshift white plastic wrap. I supposed it was his own creation. To his credit, every year, those roses bloomed. And each year they were bolder and brighter, with ever more buds. I can assure you it is not because we have green thumbs.

I had once seen Mama clip the lavender lilac bushes on the side of our house into an arrangement. She wrapped the stems in a soaking-wet paper towel and then covered the towel in tin foil. I brought them to my second-grade teacher, Miss Sharretts. Every time I passed by her desk, I stopped to smell the lilacs. In this memory, I decided to cut the roses and put them in miniature vases throughout the house. It soon became a tradition and all summer long we had something fresh, something homegrown, something vibrant in our home. We sometimes brought bouquets of our roses to Mama's grave. I have always pictured them in my wedding bouquet.

LOSING HAIR

One of the times Mama was home from the hospital, we went out to lunch with one of her childhood friends and her family. It was a breezy fall day, and we were in the parking lot of TGIFriday's. Mama was wearing one of her favorite Liz Claiborne sweaters. It was bright red. Mama didn't typically wear such attention-catching colors, but she was having a good week. As we were hugging everyone goodbye, I noticed a clump of auburn-brown hair stuck to my Mama's shoulder. I walked behind Mama and strategically pulled the hair free from her shirt, letting it blow away in the wind behind her so that she wouldn't see. It was Mama's hair. *This* was cancer. I never saw a lump or a real life tumor. Instead I saw things like this. Mama warned us that this would happen, but I didn't think it was fair that she had to hurt so badly both on the inside and on the outside.

A few weeks later, Mama and Daddy surprised us by announcing an early-dismissal from our elementary school. The principal's voice came over the loudspeaker in our classroom, and I jumped for joy at the news that we would be leaving school early! My brother and I ran up the long hallway to hug Mama and Daddy when we saw them waiting in the principal's office.

We were going to the wig parlor. Mama had been preparing us since day one that she would eventually need to get a wig to disguise her head as her hair began to fall out due to the chemo. I asked her if she would have to wear the wig all the time. She said that it would be temporary until the cancer was gone and then her hair would grow back. She explained that sometimes the new hair, after cancer, grows back in with a different texture or color even! She said she hoped there was no more gray and laughed.

We were getting used to Mama's balding head even though it was quite obvious she was very self-conscious about her new appearance. Today, as I have a husband of my own, I wonder how she questioned her femininity and beauty in her husband's eyes. Mama didn't want to embarrass us kids, I heard her say once on the phone. I smoothed my hair with the palm of my hand, wishing there was some way I could give her mine.

Daddy ushered us into the parlor, and I noticed hundreds of wigs hanging from the walls. There were ceramic busts sporting untamed wigs. Mama and Daddy talked to the saleslady as we clung to their sides in this strange place. After a few moments I carefully picked up a long light brown wig from the counter and held it up to Mama. She studied it for a moment and told me it was perfect. The owner of the shop was eccentric and sweet. When Daddy nervously asked her how much the one I was holding cost, she walked over to me and whispered in my ear to tell Daddy it was an early Christmas present from Santa. My Daddy's eyes glistened.

Mama sat in the vintage beauty parlor chair facing the mirror as the lady placed the wig on Mama's balding scalp. We sat behind them on a wooden bench under a large set of bay windows. Mama blushed when she saw herself in the mirror sporting the long straight locks. I had never seen Mama with long hair. Mama's clothes were too big for her now. When she leaned forward to put the apron on, I caught a glimpse of blue marker residue near her collarbone. I had seen those markings before. It was from her radiation treatments.

The saleslady began swiftly snipping and cutting the hair until it looked exactly like Mama's favorite hairstyle. We all sat on the wooden bench and watched as Mama's self-consciousness began to fade. She could get used to this. It wasn't as bad as she thought it would be. She wouldn't even have to wash her hair. We all walked over to the pizza parlor across the street for lunch. I saw Mama admire her reflection in the glass windows. She looked beautiful. What a blessing.

MANILA

We were driving on Union Deposit Road in our green minivan. The van had outlets that you could plug your headphones into so that two different radio stations could be played simultaneously. My brother and I always fought over who would get to use the headphones. But that day, it was just Mama and me. There was a large manila envelope resting on the dashboard. It was reflecting in the windshield, making it appear to double in size.

Suddenly, Mama reached over to the dashboard and turned down the radio. She didn't look at me. I looked at her. She took a deep breath and exhaled. I flashbacked to the conversation we had on the couch a few days earlier. She proceeded to tell me that the doctor we had just seen was examining a lump in her breast. When she said the word breast, I cringed. I hated talking about puberty and embarrassing things associated with it. She told me that everything was going to be okay. I just stared ahead at the road, desperately trying to hide my horror. I didn't ask any questions, but she continued to talk anyway. She said that she was going to see a lot of really good doctors.

Mama took me with her to her first chemo treatment. I got to sit and play games and hold her hand while she sat in a tan leather La-Z-Boy recliner. She kept her eyes on me while they stuck her plump skin with the needles. As the weeks went on, her plump skin turned sallow. It was bruised, yellowing, and paper thin. She flinched when the nurse unwrapped the needles. I made cheesecakes for all of the doctors on the seventh floor of the hospital. Mama had circled the recipe and wrote "great" in cursive next to it in the Better Homes Cook Book. It was the best thing I knew how to bake.

REALITY

I don't think people expected much out of me when she passed away. When the frozen meals turned into a pile of empty Tupperware containers, the truth of the situation set in. My Daddy didn't know the first thing about raising two children, much less an adolescent daughter. As far as I was concerned, my Daddy worked and my Mama stayed home and cooked dinner for us. Sometimes we would go shopping and she would hide the expensive bags in the trunk until Daddy went upstairs. To be completely honest, I don't really remember much of my Daddy before my Mama got sick. I refer to these parts of my life as before cancer and after cancer.

Many blessings were bestowed upon my family during the year of her illness. In fact, I dare say the blessings outweighed the tragedies, numerically at least. Most of the time, any and all strength granted by the blessings was veiled by the absolute heartbreak that accompanied the tragedies. For instance, the year that my Mama got sick, we all started saying "I love you" to each other when we parted ways. Religiously. Before cancer, I would squirm away from her hugs at the bus stop. After cancer, I never missed an opportunity to tell her I loved her. I hoped she would ask for a hug. We knew her days were numbered. I never had the courage to ask Mama if she thought she was going to die, or what did she want me to do if she did, or how would I know she was looking down at me? I feared that speaking such words would surely bring them to life. We could have worked out some sort of signal, a code or something that would transcend heaven. Instead, we lived. We lived for each day. The future was not something we wanted to rush.

It was a night like no other. Our whole evening routine was different. Mama spent most of the evening sitting on the steps in the dark hallway talking on the cordless phone. Daddy came home from work earlier than usual. Dinner was already on the table, but instead of sitting down at the kitchen table, Daddy called us all into the family room.

We all sat on the pastel-colored couch. For the first time ever, I noticed the redness in my Mama's tired eyes. All week, Mama and Daddy had been acting unusual. I heard them arguing downstairs in the evenings. I was bracing myself for the announcement that they were getting a divorce. You know, like all the other kids' families were doing. I would have been okay with that. Instead, my Mama told us that she was sick. Cancer, she called it. She would need a lot of hugs and kisses to get better. But she would, definitely, get better. There were a lot of good doctors ready to help her. I was still.

I didn't know much about cancer except that it tasted like a dirty word. My initial thought was that I would be on my own one day. My mother would abandon us. Though I couldn't begin to fathom the depths of sadness I would soon experience, I felt the tears coming on. Daddy never knew the right answers to any of my math homework problems. Consequently, I had stopped asking him in third grade. Mama leaned forward to embrace us, and I inhaled her sweet, clean scent. Elizabeth Taylor's White Diamonds.

When I felt her tears dampen my face, I pulled away avoiding her glance. I took off for the kitchen door, leaving everyone on the couch behind me. I made this about me. I grabbed the cordless phone that was charging in the garage off the wall and I dialed Abby's number. Abby was my best friend who lived five houses down the street from me.

By the way Mrs. Eldridge answered, I had a feeling Abby already knew what I was about to tell her. We met in the usual spot, the sidewalk halfway between both of our houses. Neither of us had put our jackets on. Abby's hair was damp. I was barefoot. The orange sun had almost dropped from the sky. I told Abby my Mama had cancer and then we hugged each other. I ran all the way back to my house and straight up to my bedroom, slamming the door behind me. I pulled a blanket over my head and started sobbing uncontrollably. Hiccups, snot, and tears smeared into the belly of my teddy bear. Later that night, my Mama picked the lock on my door and rocked me to sleep.

MASTER PLAN

I have always done everything exactly according to a master plan. The irony is that I created the rules I would follow. Like I said before, nobody really expected very much out of me considering my circumstances. I would be average. I was middle-class and had a good start in life, but would, undoubtedly, turn out like every other average girl: drop out of athletics, probably have a baby kind of young, date a bunch of losers, and never leave the suburbs. However, whatever my Mama managed to jam into me in the ten short years she had me must have stuck. Because I was not an average girl by any means. At least, I was certain I was not normal. Throughout the years, I've come to learn that some of the most special, most extraordinary women have come from motherless backgrounds. This both comforts and intrigues me.

My friends' parents easily took a liking to me, and I sometimes preferred talking with them. I wanted to gather wisdom from parents. I wanted my friends' moms to treat me special like they did their daughters. I just craved mothering. I was Parents' Pick in my high school year book, a category for someone whom everyone's parents like. Maybe my friends' parents felt bad for me. Or maybe they were surprised that I was different. To the public, I was the face of our family. My Daddy was sacrificing his prime years in order to raise us the best way he knew how. I realized my behavior would be viewed as a direct product of his efforts. I wanted him to know he was doing a good thing and to see that his hard work was paying off.

Then there was puberty. A few months before Mama died, I had come back from a friend's birthday-party sleepover when I noticed something was not right. I stood upstairs in my bedroom staring down at the flamingo striped fabric. My heart was shaking and I thought I was going to die. I debated keeping it a secret. But then I realized that if I didn't tell my Mama now, I might never have the chance. Somehow I knew this was important to her. I heard her downstairs transferring the groceries into the refrigerator. Nobody else was home; it was just us. I walked out of the bedroom and tiptoed over to the balcony. I sprinted back to my room. I walked over again, peeked down to see if she was there and then walked back to my room yelling at myself in my head to just get it over with. I was so embarrassed.

Finally, I marched back out to the balcony and softly called out her name. My voice cracked. I asked her to come upstairs. She dropped what she was doing and walked up the stairs. I stood at the top of the steps and told her what had happened in as few words as possible. It felt like I had swallowed a bag of marbles and they were lodged in my throat. I couldn't look her in the eye. I told her I thought something was wrong, and I cried. She stared at the garment and then sat down slowly on my plaid comforter. She had worn her wig that day to pick me up from my friend's birthday party, and she looked very young and pretty. I folded my arms in front of my developing body and started crying. She looked so caught off guard. She was speechless. She put her hand on my back and sat me on the bed. Tears started dripping down her pale cheeks. And then a smile made its way across her face as she gazed at me with the tears in her eyes. I just sat there wide-eyed and embarrassed.

She told me I was becoming a woman. I didn't want to become a woman. Especially when I was the only woman in the sixth grade. Why did this have to happen now? She told me I should feel lucky; all the girls will be jealous. I will even get breasts soon. I told her I didn't want or need them. She told me that it might not be the real thing and it might not really come for a while, I would just have to wait and see. I hated when she used those puberty terms. She took a Lisa Frank pencil out from my desk and circled the date on my Kitten calendar.

I made her swear not to tell my Daddy or anyone else, for that matter. It was our little secret. That night she took me to Olive Garden with one of her neighbor friends. At the table, she asked the neighbor if we could stop at the drugstore on the way home. She whispered something in her ear. I saw the lady stare at me and flash a knowing grin. I wanted to melt into a puddle and seep through the seat. At the drugstore, Mama went inside and bought me pads. That box was the last thing my Mama bought me.

After cancer, I had no way of getting these types of "girl" things. I couldn't be sure whether or not Mama had honored my desperate plea to not tell my Daddy. So I tried to make the few supplies last. I found an extra box in her bathroom. And one time my grandma bought me a box, even though I never asked her to. Whenever that time came around, I threw out the garments so that my Daddy would not see them in the laundry. One morning when my Daddy came to wake me up he kneeled next to my bed to kiss me good morning and looked into the trash bin and saw all of the colored fabric. He was mortified. He simply told me I could do my own laundry if I wanted. That is when I started doing laundry.

I would spend hours poring over teen magazines to try to figure things out ahead of time. I couldn't afford to be caught off guard again. If something like that was going to happen again, I needed to know and prepare. The magazines were my only source of information. Sometimes I would share the explicit information I was learning with my friends and they would go home and ask their parents what certain terms meant. Then I would get in trouble.

INDEPENDENCE

I gained a lot of what I understand as independence before cancer. The remaining bits and whatever was left, I certainly earned after cancer. Mama always treated me as though she knew something special about me. I guess that's just why mamas can't be replaced. Though I can't recall aha moments, even in hindsight, Mama must have jammed a lot of lessons into me before and during cancer because I had already made up my mind that cancer was not going to unravel the marvelous work she put into raising our family. And, when I decide and commit to something, it always transpires. Sometimes I am saddened by my ambush of independence. I wanted to be a big girl. I needed to be a big girl.

It was springtime. Mama was in the hospital. Daddy, my brother, and I were at home. It was a bright sunshiny morning. The breeze was whipping the curtains in the formal dining room and flowing throughout the house. Daddy kept the windows open at night when it was cool out. We had spent the latter part of the evening at the hospital visiting Mama. I think she was having an important surgery this morning. It was one of so many, but with each one you just never knew when it would be the last. She was getting a device implanted in her body that would act as a port for the IVs that were always strung around her like Christmas lights. Oh, the irony. She needed it because at this point her fragile arms were so pricked and badly bruised that the nurses weren't able to find her veins anymore. The fact this device was permanent only further confirmed my suspicion that Mama wasn't going to be leaving the hospital any time soon. I had purposely left my homework at home so I would not have to do it at the hospital. The looming homework assignment was to write a story about a St. Patrick's Day leprechaun.

Daddy was making us dippy eggs in the kitchen. Every morning he set out our Flintstones vitamin, toothbrush with toothpaste already applied, and a full-out breakfast. He even went as far as packing our lunches and writing notes on the napkins, just like Mama did. I wonder if she asked him to do that. I was in the den typing up my assignment. I was proud of my typing skills at such a young age. I was the fastest typist in Mr. Yanchuk's computer class.

When I was satisfied with my hurried assignment, I yelled into the kitchen for Daddy to come proofread what I had written so far. Pap had been opening the office in the mornings so Daddy could get us off to school. He paced over, wearing his blue work uniform and faded blue socks, his cologne preceding his entrance. He was scrubbing a stain from my brother's baseball pants. He barely looked at the screen and told me it looked great. That was not what I wanted to hear. That's not how Mama did it. I pointed to a paragraph that I didn't particularly like. He suggested that I add a paragraph about a pot of gold. He said something about lucky charms. He just didn't get it. I pouted in the computer chair and stomped my feet so that he would hear it as he walked out into the kitchen. I told him that I abhorred his idea. I wanted him to tell me how to make it sound more professional. Where should I add paragraphs? His advice was so off point. Mama always came up with lovely scenes and ideas that she would ramble out loud and then I would type them in as fast as I could. I yelled at him that he didn't know what he was doing. He told me to go brush my teeth.

I stomped my feet in the rolling computer chair, and I asked him for Mama's hospital room number. I had seen Mama stomp her feet one time. I thought maybe I could subconsciously manipulate Daddy into being sympathetic. He straightened his voice and told me she would be sleeping and not to wake her. I pretended that I didn't hear a word he said as I marched past him in the kitchen and grabbed the cordless phone from the wall. For greater effect, I pushed my plate across the table and knocked over the glass of orange juice. I wanted the noise but not the mess. Whatever. I dialed the hospital number from memory and asked for Mama's room number. Mama answered, and in between sobs, I told her that Daddy wasn't helping me and I only had a few minutes to write the story about the leprechaun and everyone else in my class was going to have a great story and mine was awful.

Mama told me to calm down. She sounded tired, though. Weak. It struck me that nobody could take her place. She, in her illness, could not even take her place. Nobody, save myself, could help me. I sat in front of the computer screen, with a hardened face, and reluctantly printed out the paper.

That morning, as I read the story out loud in front of my class, I was ashamed of worrying my Mama. When I finished presenting, I sat back down at my desk and wondered if Mama had made it out of her surgery alive. Would they interrupt my school day to tell me she had died? Would Nan or Daddy knock on our classroom door to get us? Every time our overhead speaker crackled I held my breath . . . preparing myself for the worst. The other students' papers were awful. Daddy. He couldn't replace Mama. He just didn't get it. And yet I was so sorry I had pointed that out to him.

READING

Daddy used to tell me Mama insisted that anyone who put me to sleep must read to me, at the very least, one storybook. This was important to her. She always liked to read. I tried reading from her collection, but the books were far beyond my years. I found out later that before she was married, she was a paralegal. So it was only natural that she was the best with spelling and homework.

My favorite childhood book was "Goodnight Moon." We could never just read it straight through. I insisted on pointing out the socks hanging by the fireplace and every other detail in that room. Mama's favorite book was "Love You Forever." Without fail, Mama was always in tears by the time we got to the last few pages. I found this to be amusing. When she saw me giggling, Mama would just smile back at me and wipe the corners of her eyes with the back of her palm and smooth my hair. She would kiss me on the forehead and say, "One day, honey."

Daddy tried to uphold her academic example. In fact, he taught me how to spell my first big word. He was picking out clothes for me to wear to preschool when we lived in the old townhouse. I must have been about four. I asked him what the hardest word he knew how to spell was. So he told me it was the word k-n-o-w-l-e-d-g-e. We practiced it over and over that morning and the next morning and in the car to school until I had mastered it. None of my friends would know there was a silent k. Then I asked him for an even harder word. So he taught me to spell s-p-a-g-h-e-t-t-i.

In elementary school, I was invited to compete in the spelling bee. Daddy was so proud. He would stand in the kitchen holding the official spelling bee handbook in one hand while spreading peanut butter and jelly on bread with his other hand. Whenever he asked me a word that I did not know, I would yell at him and tell him they would never ask me that. He never let me get away with that. On the day of the competition, Daddy and Nan sat in the back of the cafeteria at one of the folding lunch tables. This was after cancer. If it was before cancer, Mama would have been there too. She noticeably wasn't.

I made it through four rounds. It was between two other contestants who were in the sixth grade and me. I took my place on the stage and the judge asked me to spell the word m-o-n-g-o-o-s-e. The smug smile slipped from my face as I stared at the wire grid of the microphone and the silent audience before me. I noticed Daddy and Nan smiling widely as if their smiles could somehow telepathically spell the word for me. It didn't work. I got it wrong. I was so disappointed with myself. After the bell chimed, I turned around and walked off the stage pouting.

Upon entering the speckled-tile hallway, I fought back tears. It was then that I reminded myself that this didn't need to be the biggest achievement in my life — there would be bigger opportunities for me. I took a deep breath, straightened my posture, and wiped my face with my palms. I returned to my class section in the audience and sat on the cafeteria floor. I was not good at failing. I avoided Daddy and Nan's smiles. I would never forget how to spell mongoose. Ironically, at Christmas, my other grandma bought me a purple-and-silver bicycle. Across the steel beam, in thick white block letters was the brand Mongoose. I cringed.

Amanda M. Harding

The Woman of the House

Part Seven
HOW OTHERS REACT

The Woman of the House

HOW OTHERS REACT

When people found out Mama had cancer, they were heartbroken. Their generosity and willingness to help our family was overwhelming. It was comforting knowing that so many people loved us enough to reach out to us in our time of need. As the cancer progressed, I noticed people becoming more and more concerned when they asked how Mama was doing. I could see the worry and pity in their eyes. It was a sixth sense I had acquired.

After Mama passed away, people generally acted uncomfortable around us. There are several people who stand out in my mind as going above and beyond to make me feel normal and loved, but the majority of people were at a complete loss as to how to behave toward us.

When Mother's Day rolled around, my friends would accidentally ask me what I was getting for my mom. They would quickly recover and say sorry and change the subject. New friends would ask if my mama could give them a ride home from basketball practice. No, but my grandma can.

Whenever the situation came up where I needed to address the fact that I did not have a living mama, I had to make a split decision as to whether or not it was worth investing the time and energy to explain. Did I feel like dealing with the long silence and seeing the other person frozen, speechless, left searching for the right thing to say? Most of the time I chose not to elaborate on the situation, but occasionally I would let the person know that my mama had passed away and I would hope they didn't ask too many questions so I did not get emotional, although sometimes I wished people asked me more questions about her. Sometimes I wanted to tell them.

GROWING OLD

One evening my Nan was at the hospital visiting with Mama. Nan made a casual complaint about the wrinkles around her eyes and that she was getting old. She looked over at Mama expecting a laugh, and Mama, half asleep and to no one in particular, dreamily replied, "I wish I could grow old . . ." I've never heard Nan complain about her wrinkles since.

ART TEACHERS

In elementary school all of my teachers knew that my mother had died. Though it sometimes felt like it, I actually did *not* have a sign on my forehead stating that I was a Motherless Daughter. Nonetheless, I was hesitant about the transition into junior high school. Certainly the topic of our parents would arise at some point, as it always does when you have small classes, and I did not want to have to confront the topic in front of my new peers. I knew many kids whose parents were divorced or who didn't know their fathers, but I felt so different. Death seemed so taboo. Once I was afraid that if people knew my Mama died, they would be afraid to hang out with me. I sometimes wondered if there was some way to put an asterisk by my name so when the teachers called roll on the first day of class, they would see the notation and remember that I was special.

In high school I always favored art classes. Being creative was liberating. One day I was cleaning a paintbrush in the stainless steel sink with my back to our teacher when I overheard a conversation about breast cancer being formulated. It was not uncommon to talk about provocative topics in our art classes. I couldn't control my lips as they blurted out, "My Mama had cancer." My teacher and her companion looked over to me with sorry faces and swiftly responded, "I'm sorry to hear that, but she's okay now, right?" they asked, finishing the sentence with certainty.

"No. She died." The lady looked like she swallowed a bird. The soft picture lighting in the room couldn't disguise her colorless face. She was embarrassed. I wanted her sympathy, wanted her to know how much it hurt, glad someone finally knew, glad that she understood the severity of what a loss like that means. This is the life of a motherless daughter. I feel cheated and incomplete without her physical presence at all times.

From that day on, my art teacher looked in my eyes more deeply when she spoke to me. One day, not long after the incident, I was standing in front of an easel staring at the blank canvas when she came up behind me and said, "Feel the fear and do it anyways." And one stroke at a time, I would harness in all the fear and then I would push my brush to the fabric and begin. Each and every stroke went like that.

FORTY

One day I was telling Mama's sister, my aunt, what I had been up to my last year of college, and she replied very seriously, "Honey, don't try and do everything before you're 40." I was sincerely offended.

I wanted her to say something more along the lines of, "Your mama would be so proud of you." Later, I pondered what my aunt would have said if I really delved into the lengthy list of goals I set for myself and was hell bent on achieving. I wondered if her response was something she had once told Mama, too, or if it was something Mama had once told her. Or maybe it was something Mama had wanted her to tell me. Regardless, the statement has been like a peculiar weed inside my head. I have picked it up a thousand times and had a look, each time putting it away again. I am unable to grasp the complexity, the wisdom, the probably well-meaning nature of her statement. It perpetually perplexes me. Gorgeous, it's been patiently waiting for me to find a place where it makes sense.

For now, it does not make sense. Mama was only thirty-seven when she died.

I was never interviewed by Oprah or on the Today Show begging a doctor to find a cure for cancer. I never publicly pleaded for anyone to cure Mama. Yet I did not understand why her death was not on the front page of the Patriot-News? At the time, I would have been embarrassed if this was the case. Cancer was humiliating. It was not just a tumor; it was a disease that attacked a family. Cancer is humbling.

Of course, in our neighborhood, school, and community her absence was being recognized. Our house was the one without a mom. The wreaths hanging from our front door would be a little lopsided, a little outdated. Our curtains might not match our dishrags in the kitchen. The kids inside might not have perfectly combed hair. But that would be it. Those tiny little details would be the only clues that we did not have a mama. I would make certain of this. I realized that a really big part of me wanted to receive recognition for things. To make sure that I was not caught "doing nothing."

DEAR DIARY

October, 30 1998

Dear Diary,

> *Today was a good but terrible day! Abby told me that Melody said that my mom*

This sentence sits open-ended in a page in my childhood journal. At the time, I was petrified that if I continued to finish the sentence it would come true. I hated that my friends were talking behind my back about Mama's life. Her life. My Mama. I hated that what they knew was probably true. I hated being left out. I hated that they didn't even have the slightest clue what I was going through.

Mama passed away on November 9, 1998.

Amanda M. Harding

The Woman of the House

Part Eight

REMEMBERING MAMA

The Woman of the House

REMEMBERING MAMA

When I was up at bat, I would always think of Mama. I wanted her to be in the stands watching me hit a homerun or slide into second base. I wanted to see the pride on her face when I got my name in the newspaper or accomplished something great. I found ways to stay connected with her by talking to her often. I kind of knew what she would say. I've had to re-evaluate my relationship with her as I grow older. I still think of her when I hear Sara McLachlan's "Angel" or Mariah Carey's "Butterfly" on the radio. I imagine it's Mama's way of sending me a sign. I pray for her, look at old pictures of her, wear her rings, and my handwriting is similar to hers. One of the greatest compliments I can receive is hearing that she would be proud of me or that I look like her or that I do something she used to do.

LAZY MAN'S LOAD

One night, before cancer, it was my turn to clear the table after dinner. I scooped up all the plates in one arm and spent an excessive amount of time trying to strategically place the last bowl on top. From the other room, Mama shouted to me that her Daddy called that a "lazy man's load." It didn't stop me from my task at hand, but I did like knowing that my Pappy Bruce coined this term. I thought it was funny and very truthful. I often hear Mama saying this to me in my own kitchen.

WORK

When we were younger, while Mama and Daddy were at work, my brother and I went to a popular daycare center close to our house. Getting out of the house in the mornings was hectic for Mama. One day Mama found a pair of her silk panties statically clung to the inside of my brother's jacket. Or there was the time I dropped the gallon of milk while trying to get it out of the refrigerator. The small lobby of the daycare center had a sign-in book and a bowl of individually wrapped sesame pretzel sticks. While Mama signed us in, I stuffed the pretzels into my coat pockets. Mama would punch a code into a keypad, which set off a loud buzzer signaling that we could enter. She put our belongings in our cubby space, removed our jackets, and kissed us goodbye. Every day.

In the late afternoon, the daycare center would empty into the fenced-in playground for recess until each child was picked up and taken home. Every night I would stand at the playground castle's highest peak, the spot right in front of the yellow slide. I could see the maroon tanbark below and smell the discarded cooking oil wafting from the grocery store a hundred yards behind the daycare center. From my vantage point, I would study the cars in traffic, never certain which way Mama actually came from. I played this game of trying to find her car to soothe my incessant anxiety over whether or not she would come to pick me up. I was always alone up there looking for her.

I've often wondered if children have an instinct about their mamas that only they can perceive, having grown from their mama's womb. Have we witnessed something of her that no one else can sense? Did I know early on that I needed to savor her. Did I know? On another hand, I sometimes think Mama struggled with her own father's sudden death and somehow imparted this anxiety to my psyche at a young age.

NEW CAR

One month before Mama passed, she was given permission by all of her doctors to come home for the weekend. She insisted that she wanted to be in her home with us. Daddy had several meetings with the doctors before they reluctantly agreed. Daddy told us that he had a surprise for Mama. All of a sudden, a big truck came down the street and pulled up in front of our house. On the back was a trailer carrying a brand-new, gold BMW. The truck driver lowered the trailer to the ground. Mama started crying when she realized it was for her. All of our neighbors started clapping and cheering as they watched her smile. It was one of the sweetest gestures Daddy had ever done for her. She was so frail and weak, but we all got in the car and she opened the sunroof and drove us around the neighborhood.

There was even a cell phone mounted on the dash. By the time we got back to our driveway, she was exhausted and had to go inside and hook up the oxygen tubes to her face. On Sunday Mama had to go back to the hospital. I remember standing in the driveway with Nan as Daddy backed out of the driveway with Mama in the passenger seat. She was crying as she waved to us. She knew it would be the last time she would ever see her home. The home they built their family in. The home she raised her children in. Our home.

When I got my license, I knew Daddy was going to give me Mama's car. It had been kept in the garage for six years. We only drove it on the weekends. The first place I drove to was the cemetery. I couldn't wait to sit and talk with Mama in peace. I parked my car on an angle and shined my headlights toward her grave. It was nice to be able to savor this moment by myself.

When Daddy would take us to the cemetery, it was always very brief. We could not bear to be there for too long. The three-mile radius surrounding the cemetery always made my stomach uneasy. When I was in junior high, our track team would go for long runs, often overlapping this radius. I always dreaded this route as I was forced to act like everything was normal when clearly it was not. While everyone else's moms were waiting in their SUVs to take us home from practice, mine was lying in a casket beneath the very dirt we were running on.

Even when I was driving with Daddy and our errands took us through that part of town, I would never mention anything about Mama. I never asked to go to the cemetery, even though it was all I wanted. I wanted to sit in silence and weep and bring flowers the way actresses did in the movies. When we did go, usually after church, we would gradually move from the car, careful not to look at each other's faces. Daddy always led the way. We would tiptoe down the hill toward her plot, slowly and somberly.

I had always envisioned cemeteries with large grave stones like Pappy Bruce's, and so I was disappointed when, instead, Mama's was just a small plaque built into the ground. Daddy always kneeled down in front of her plaque. He took out the towels and bottle of water he always brought with him. He would carefully clean the leaves and grass off of the gray, marble edges until they glistened. We would stand behind him in the glow of the headlights, wrestling away tears. In the summer, we brought roses from our garden.

Sometimes I would see bouquets of flowers that I did not recognize. I liked knowing that other people still remembered and visited her. I loosened the vase from its stand to clean it in the same methodical way I watched Daddy do for all these years. I noticed a yellow piece of legal paper all folded up. I was confused, not sure if it was disrespectful to open it. I did so anyway, and it simply read, "Thank you." It was written in my father's handwriting. My eyes watered. I folded it back up and returned it to its resting place. I have always wondered what it was that he was thanking Mama for.

STUBBORN

When I was just in second grade, Mama gave me a yellow cloth scrunchie to wear in my ponytail for the yearbook picture. I had been growing out my bangs and so they stuck up high in my ponytail without the scrunchie. I kept telling her I hated it, but she managed to get me out of the house with it still intact. When it was my time to sit on the little stool and get my photo taken, I pulled out the scrunchie and the photographer snapped the picture. When the big envelopes came in a few weeks later, Mama was devastated. She told me I should be embarrassed to give out the pictures. She was right, as usual.

In the months before cancer, I begged Mama to let me redecorate my bedroom since Abby's parents had just painted her bedroom yellow. Mama promised me that I could. A few weeks into cancer Mama surprised me and took me to Home Depot to pick out paint. I insisted on a sky-blue color, and she allowed me to get it even though she made it very obvious that it was not her first choice. Then we drove to Kmart so I could pick out a wallpaper border. I really wanted this floral Martha Stewart border, but I hated that the background was a creamy-beige color. I wanted it to be white so that it would match the sky-blue paint.

Mama asked all of the sales associates if there were any without the beige border. There were none. One employee called all the Kmarts in our area. Nothing. I threw a tantrum in the store, and so Mama bought the beige colored border and spent hours sitting in the oversized living-room chair cutting out each little intricate flower from the border so that I would have it just the way I wanted it. I want to cry now as I relive that. I was so selfish and stubborn, and I let her waste her precious time doing *that*. I am still ashamed of myself.

ERR

I remember playing Scrabble when we spent the weekend at Grandma's house. Everyone knew Mama was really good at Scrabble, so they were always out to beat her. I remember lying down in my pajamas next to Mama with my head propped up on my hands while she organized her letters. When it was her turn, she played the word E-R-R. My aunt made Mama go get the Webster's dictionary from Grandma's office so they could verify that was a "real word." Mama assured them that it was. I didn't know what it meant, but I sure hoped Mama was right. She was.

Anytime I have the chance to use that word, I do and I am brought back to this sweet memory.

PICTURES

I wonder if Mama will age to what would be her accurate age in my mind. I can't imagine her older than the age she died, but at some point she will have to do so in my mind even though she never did physically. How will that happen?? I imagine what she would look like in today's styles, with graying hair. And I just can't. To me she will always be thirty-seven years old wearing her favorite, now outdated outfits. I picture her in the kitchen the way it used to be, before we remodeled it. I picture the Pfaltzgraff dinnerware she was so proud of. The new cups and silverware she bought. She had waited months for them to go on sale.

I wish there were more photos. I have an insatiable appetite for lost memories. We have many photos from our childhood, but Mama was always the one behind the lens. Those are my only memories. For some reason, all of the other images, the ones I used to have in my mind, have faded. The more I try to focus my mind's eye on her face and her features, the blurrier her image becomes. It is so frustrating to only have a few images of a woman I was surrounded by for the first ten years of my life.

I have anxiety when it comes to capturing memories. I never want to forget things. One of Mama's assignments from her counselor before she passed away was to organize our family photos into albums. Mama had put all of our pictures in piles in cardboard boxes. She completed several albums. After her death, the box sat in her closet . . . unfinished. Sometimes I imagine life is like stacking a bunch of pictures on top of each other and being able to feel the presence of everyone at once.

MY BIBLE

I got my first Bible from Sunday school class after confirmation. We had to recite Psalm 23 by memory and then we would get our names etched in gold at the bottom. Mama was so proud of me. She showed me her Bible that evening so we could compare them. It was white and shiny and it had a neat zipper that enclosed the pages. It had gold cursive writing etched into the front. I always wanted to bring it with me instead of my plain shiny black one. The first pages had a note from Grandma and Pappy Bruce on her birthday. I can't remember if she had ever written in her Bible. I wonder what passages spoke to her. No, I never asked her.

BRACES

A few years before cancer, Mama got braces on her teeth. She was always bothered by her bottom tooth that was just a tiny bit crooked. I used to tease her about her crooked tooth. I remember it seemed funny that my thirty-something-year-old

Mama had braces. She wore the clear bands so it was not as noticeable. She wore them for about a year, and she was so happy with the results.

Two years after cancer, my brother and I went to the dentist and got braces for the gap between our front teeth. We chose pink, blue, and sometimes multicolored bands for ours. Eventually, we had picture-perfect smiles.

Then a strange thing happened. And when I say weird or strange, I am usually reminded that it is a God thing. When I was twenty-three years old, I noticed that my bottom tooth was tilting slightly to the side. Great, I thought to myself. I would have to get braces or something again. It's probably happening because I never wore my retainer. I didn't pay much attention to it until one day I was standing at my apartment sink analyzing my slightly crooked tooth in the mirror when I had a flashback of Mama's smile. I began to smile. Tears welled in my eyes. I ran my finger over the tooth. Sure enough, I could feel the difference. If Mama were here, I can imagine her laughing. I love it.

MAMA'S CURSIVE

When I was in third grade, I learned to write in cursive. I would envision Mama's loopy, yet clean, cursive writing on the little note pads she had scattered throughout the house. I did not like the uniformed cursive writing they were teaching us at school. We had to write on the extra-large lined paper that had a dashed line running through the middle so that you could accurately differentiate the height between lower-case and capital letters. When I pushed the yellow pencil to the paper, I was never satisfied with the shape that resulted. I wanted my handwriting to look as sophisticated as Mama's. Mama helped me practice my cursive each night. She even showed me shortcuts, like making a little squiggle to represent the word "and." She helped me develop my very first signature.

Toward the end of third grade, Mrs. Ellis had asked us to bring a piece of stationery and an envelope to class for a special project. Mama had taken me to the Hallmark store the night before and helped me pick out my first set of stationery. I chose a pale yellow set that was embellished with orange and gold butterflies. I couldn't wait to bring it to class and show Abby. Yellow was our favorite color. I had never considered that something as simple as stationery would somehow foster such a memorable bond in my heart.

We had also been asked to choose the night before a person to write our letter to. The objective was to practice our cursive writing in a real-world scenario. After coming up short of anyone old enough to actually receive mail, I went to Mama. She suggested writing to my Great-grandmother

Taylor. I knew Mama and Great-grandmother were very close because every time we visited her, they would stay up late and talk by themselves for hours — or what seemed like hours. Mama assured me that Great-grandmother would love to hear from me.

I sat at my desk and addressed the envelope to Great-grandmother Taylor, just like Mama showed me. Mrs. Ellis then had us take out our stationery and place it at an angle on our desk so that our handwriting would be perfectly slanted. I started off very carefully, in huge, cursive letters, "Dear Great-grandmother Taylor." The letters looked lovely under the little butterflies. I went on to tell Great-grandmother how I was in Mrs. Ellis' third grade class and I was practicing my cursive. I told her about our hamster Brownie that just had twelve babies and my new goldfish and about how my brother lost his front tooth because I pushed him into the couch. Once I was satisfied, I folded the stationery into thirds and placed it inside the envelope. I sealed it shut and raised my hand for Mrs. Ellis' approval. She came over and placed a stamp in the right-hand corner. I was the first one to finish.

I raced home from the bus stop every day in anticipation for Great-grandmother to write me back. A week later, I opened the mailbox to see an envelope addressed to Miss Amanda! A letter, for me! Great-grandmother had written back to me in cursive too. For the rest of the school year, Mrs. Ellis gave us the option to stay inside for the first half of recess when she would help us write back to our new pen pals. I always stayed and wrote back the very next day. I looked forward to Great-grandmother's stories about her cats and her garden. I liked answering the questions she asked me. She made me feel older and important. Mama told me Great Grandmother thought I had lovely handwriting and that I was becoming a great writer.

As the months passed, I became busy in the fourth-grade kind of way. With softball, recess, and friends taking up my thoughts and energy, the excitement of having a pen pal waned.

As the years passed, I wrote to her every so often. We didn't visit much after cancer. However, every once in a while, I would pull out my old stationery and draft a note letting her know that I was thinking of her.

A few weeks before my high school graduation, I sent her an announcement inviting her to the ceremony and a brief note, for old times' sake. Sure enough, a week later, I received a letter back in her beautiful handwriting. A pleasant surprise for me, as she was getting older. She sent her regrets that she would be unable to attend the party and slipped in a $50 bill.

At graduation, Grandma mentioned to me that Great-grandmother Taylor would love to hear from me more often and to remember to write her a thank-you note. I promised that I would. I tucked her letter away and wrote her name on the list of people I needed to write thank-you letters to when I returned from senior week in the Dominican Republic.

A week later, upon returning home from vacation, I was shuffling through the mail on the counter and I noticed a piece of paper abandoned on the countertop. It was a funeral announcement. Honoring Great-grandmother Taylor. I couldn't help but stare in disbelief. I went into my bedroom closet and pulled out the yellow stationery. I wrote her a thank-you note. In flawless cursive.

NEW CURSIVE

In high school, I adapted a new style of cursive. I made font-like a's and dotted my i's with little hearts. Oddly enough, however, every single time I made an uppercase E, I was reminded of Mama. Her name started with an E.

Then one day I was sitting in my college's academic advising office filling out the application for my first semester and something happened. I rested my ballpoint pen in the blank space where I was to fill in my major. Without hesitation, I drew a loopy, yet purposeful cursive letter E for entrepreneurship. And ever since that day, I've always wondered if I will eventually take on Mama's beautiful script.

Amanda M. Harding

The Woman of the House

Part Nine

WHAT I WISH PEOPLE HAD TOLD ME ABOUT GRIEF

The Woman of the House

Amanda M. Harding

WHAT I WISH PEOPLE HAD TOLD ME ABOUT GRIEF

My counselors probably told me all of this during our sessions, but I really wish it had sunk in more. Grief takes time. It is not different for everyone. It is the same for everyone, but we all handle it differently. We deal with it the best we can. The more equipped you are with life experiences, age, resources, the better you will be, though this isn't a guarantee either. It is important to seek out others who have been through similar situations. These people will encourage you and help you see the proverbial light at the end of the tunnel.

The hole grief digs cannot be filled by one person. Your surviving parent, a new child, or a husband will never completely fill the hole. With this in mind, I was able to stop expecting others to live up to unrealistic expectations. I was able to find peace within my own heart.

FASCINATION

Grief books always caution against the perils of idolizing a deceased loved one. I've scratched this down on my sanity checklist, which resides in my head. Perhaps I idolize my Mama by incessantly referencing her outstanding skills, some of which I really have no clear remembrance of, to my husband. I just love her. When I was in high school I would read these books, and I could literally go through each chapter and say, "Had that, yep, skipped that (fortunately!), oh, that would have helped!"

The part dealing-with-grief books leave out is that all daughters experience a rainbow of shades in which they color their mamas throughout their lives. Death just speeds that up to where all that remains is the complete rainbow. This allows a daughter to marvel at the rainbow as a whole, sans its individual fragments of color, however premature.

Amanda M. Harding

The Woman of the House

Amanda M. Harding

Part Ten

WHAT HELPS

The Woman of the House

WHAT HELPS

Counseling is very important and even better when done prior to or immediately following a loss. Through counseling I was able to learn ways to recognize and cope with my feelings. I was reminded that my feelings were okay and normal. There was nothing too shocking that the counselor hadn't heard before. I learned to journal and express my thoughts freely on paper. Keeping photographs of loved ones and good memories helps. Accomplishing things in my life always made me feel close to my Mama. I loved doing things that I knew she would have wanted me to do or things she didn't have the opportunity to do in her short life. When good things happen to me, it helps to know that my Mama may have had something to do with it. I also would regularly donate blood because Mama had received numerous blood transfusions when she was sick. Also, I firmly believe that continuing to live in the same house we grew up in was crucial to our stability.

Whenever I hear that someone has lost her mother, I recommend the book Motherless Daughters. It is the only book that I ever really read that comforted me because it was real. I keep it on my bookshelf and resort to it from time to time. Praying helps. Talking about my Mama with people who knew her helps. Spending time with family in general helps. And visiting her at the cemetery helps.

UNSTOPPABLE JOY

When I was twenty-three years old, I listened to a sermon about joy preached by Pastor Rick Blackwood in Miami. The sermon brought me to tears. I have come to understand joy transcends happiness. It is tangible. It is having a song in your heart, peace with God.

This was the missing link. This is what I needed to know all those years ago. Mama was able to endure cancer because she had a song in her heart before the cancer invaded her body. Mama knew Jesus, and she wanted to see me again one day in heaven. Sometimes I am able to smile knowing that I am, at all times, only a brief second away from heaven. At any moment I could pass away, and I know heaven is exactly where I would go. I am just a split second away from seeing Mama's sweet face again. God is so good.

CHURCH

I started going to an old Baptist church in the heart of downtown Miami. It was the most beautifully magnificent and holy church I had ever been in. The acoustics and the structure bring my heart to tears each and every Sunday. When my fiancée and I walked into it for the first time, we knew we would be married there. The first sermon we heard was about angels. It was the first time I had ever heard scripture about angels. Gazing up at the magnificently colored stained glass on the balcony, I felt angels in every nook and cranny.

I knew Mama had wanted my brother and me to continue to go to church. She had planted a seed that we would sow in her absence. She even made a point to say so in the letter she wrote us. Daddy fully supported this and took us to church every Sunday. During college, I went to many different churches in each city I lived. It wasn't until I moved to Miami — ironically, a city chock full of sin — that I really fell in love with God.

I was reminded that an angel had carried Mama upon its back from her hospital bed in Pennsylvania to heaven. I have always wondered if Mama has outstanding prayers, prayers she prayed that have yet to be fulfilled. I like to think she hand-selected my husband and prayed for us to meet and that she prayed for her future grandchildren.

There was something about the beautiful antique church and the preacher's descriptive methods that literally revealed the scriptures to me in a new light. I have never left the sanctuary without tearing up. It was the stained glass, the gilded lights, the circular structure, the ornate pews. It is a space so sacred and so sweet. The preacher actually preached scripture from the Bible. The congregation actually brought their own Bibles.

COUNSELING

When I was in sixth grade, after cancer, my father made my brother and me go to counseling. I despised talking to the old lady. I already knew what she wanted to hear. Mama started seeing her while she was sick, and then after she passed, we started going to twice weekly sessions before school. I would come to school late on those mornings. One day my teacher yelled at me for being late so often. I stood there holding my backpack in my arms as everyone in the class looked up at me from their desks. I was mortified that she was doing this to me. I cleared my voice, looked her in the eyes, and told her it was because I was going to counseling. I had never confided to any of my friends that I was seeing a therapist. Now that I am older, I want to pick that lady's brain for the secrets Mama must have shared with her.

One time I sat in the blue vinyl chair and squeezed a yellow wad of clay until it seeped through each gap between my fingers. The office was tiny and sterile, save for a few manila folders stacked on the desk. Judi, our therapist, was plain and old. She was cross-legged, turned with her back toward me, scribbling on a yellow legal pad. I always wondered if Daddy and my brother could hear me talking from the waiting room.

I was petrified that they would hear what I was saying. Or even worse, what Judi was asking me. I hated the outfit I was wearing. I knew that I did not look put together. Daddy didn't realize that I had not bought new clothes in over a year. Everything screamed that I was doing this on my own. And I knew enough to know that I did not have it right. I wore my brother's Adidas T-shirts and loose jeans. My hair was always pulled back in a low ponytail.

Judi uncrossed her legs and turned toward me. I quickly collected the seeping wad of clay and began molding it in to a soft, ladylike ball. I smoothed it gently, completely conscious of her eyes on me. I knew this was some sort of experiment. If I turned the clay into a discombobulated figure, it would mean more counseling for sure. So I began molding a miniature angel figurine. It was so cliché.

At the time, I certainly did not envision Mama as an angel. When I realized what I was doing, I was overcome with a sense of misery, knowing that I would have to walk out with this silly figure in my hand for my Daddy and my brother to witness.

Daddy kept the figurines that my brother and I made that day on top of the sugar jar in the kitchen. On display for everyone to see. Nobody would know how they got there, thank God. Sometimes when I was cleaning I would pick them up and study them. For some reason, the clay had never actually solidified. I can't begin to tell you how many times I held those figurines in my hand and violently fought the urge to squeeze them until the clay seeped through the gaps in my fingers.

Daddy always sat in the waiting room while my brother and I had our individual sessions. When my brother was with Judi, I would work on my homework or go in the bathroom and finish blow-drying my hair under the wall unit. Looking back now, from an older perspective, I don't know how Daddy managed to put toothpaste on our toothbrushes, do the laundry, cook dinner for us, pack our lunches, spend so much time with us, and keep an impeccable house. I struggled to do that just living on my own. Not to mention, he did all of this while running a highly successful business. Mama must have given him strength too. And here he was, two mornings a week, taking his young children to counseling and occasionally meeting with Judi himself.

I knew Judi had been meeting with my Mama while she was sick. I always wanted to ask her if Mama had told her anything in particular to tell me. Like a fortune. Or a wish. Judi never told me much about my Mama except that she loved me so very much and she thought I was being a wonderful help to my Daddy.

Judi always reminded me that I did not have to take my Mama's place. I was too little. Nobody expected that of me, nor did they want me to expect that of myself. Here's the thing, I had a wonderful Mama. She kept our family stable. I knew what had to be done. I never cried in counseling, although there were many days that Judi was pushing me to the brink. I really resented her for that. Did she not realize I had to go to the sixth grade afterwards? I could not have red eyes. It was already enough that everyone knew me as the girl whose mother died.

The first day that I met Judi, she asked me what I liked to do. I told her that I loved to read chapter books. She said that I should read a book called "Motherless Daughters." I raised an eyebrow at her, but kept my composure. I was being observed at all times. She asked me if I would ask my Daddy for the book. I said I would. I knew I would not. I imagined having a book like that on my bookshelf in my room and a friend seeing it.

Awkward. On the last day of our sessions together, I remember her handing me the book.

I hid the cover of the book under my arm when I walked into the waiting room and I jammed it to the bottom of my book bag, below my social studies book. When I got home from basketball practice that night, I took the book and put it in the back of my nightstand. I didn't want any of my friends to ever accidentally come across it.

I had opened the original book a few times throughout the years, but I couldn't make it through a chapter without completely breaking down. Twelve years later, I went to Barnes & Noble and purchased the book. I needed to feel like I was not alone in being motherless. The countless recollections of other motherless daughters, who had lost their mamas to a variety of different circumstances, soothed my soul. I was not alone. Other women and girls go through this every day. I know our life here on Earth is but a vapor, but going through it without your mama is really, really sad.

I do not take the lives of my Daddy and brother, or anyone else for that matter, lightly at all. Every day I question whether or not today is going to be the day that I lose someone I love. And, every so often, I conduct a checks-and-balance on my life. For instance, I ask myself: If this person were removed, would I be able to do this? That is the reality of my life. Some people get married with the security that they are going to be together for the rest of their lives. Sharing responsibilities, she does the finances, he makes the money. But, really. What happens if he were to pass away suddenly? Would her life be a shamble? I think about those things.

I have learned that other people could not and would not understand the pressure I was under. I can't blame them for not knowing. But, one day, they too will know this sorrow. I hope that when they are older they look back at the little girl, me, a friend from their childhood, and find it hard to comprehend that in my youth I handled such a tragic situation with such a mega-dose of grace. Death is part of life. I discovered this at an earlier age than most. There is not one single day that goes by in which I am not somehow reminded of this truth. I do not know, to this day, how to calculate a return on investment for the counseling I received.

The greatest thing that I took away from my counseling sessions was the act of journaling. I often lied to Judi. I felt guilty for this because I knew my Daddy was working a lot of hours to pay for the sessions. So, to make sure Daddy was getting his money's worth, I would go home and write in my own journals the truth about what I was really feeling. I would write down everything I did not tell Judi out loud. I was very self-conscious and aware of her perceptions. My young self often wrote about my future dreams and goals. One summer, I was digging through my desk drawers at home and I found one of the old journals I had hidden. I had made certain to keep them out of sight of my nosey brother and father. As I read through the pages, I realized that every single goal I had written for myself had come true. This was true for each subsequent journal. How peculiar.

Amanda M. Harding

The Woman of the House

Part Eleven

GOOD THINGS THAT COME OUT OF LOSS

The Woman of the House

GOOD THINGS THAT COME OUT OF LOSS

Had I not lost Mama, I don't know that I would ever have had the close relationship I do with my Daddy. I am Daddy's little girl. I honor and respect him so much for the role he played in our family. I am grateful for the close relationship I've fostered with my brother as well. These relationships are sacred to me. My faith has been strengthened since I lost Mama. I also know that I will be an extra good Mama to my own children since I can give them the love that Mama gave me and also so that I can do the things with them that I missed out on.

PUMPKIN ROLL

Mama's favorite dessert to bring to Thanksgiving dinner at her sister's house was

Libby's Pumpkin Roll. After cancer, I stood behind our kitchen counter and scraped the can of pumpkin into the ceramic bowl that Mama used when baking. I scooped the flower into the tan plastic measuring cup and took the edge of the butter knife and made little vertical taps over the cup before finally leveling off the excess flower in one fell swoop.

The roll part was tricky. I lined a long sheet pan, since I did not think we owned a jelly pan, with parchment paper, and I poured the batter on to it. Once it was cooked and ready to be flipped, I placed a dish towel out and sprinkled powdered sugar to keep the towel from sticking to the roll. After long and hard contemplation, I flipped the roll and wrapped it up in the towel to set in position. That is the first dish I brought to my in-laws house for Thanksgiving.

DEAR DADDY

I found this in my journal.

"Dear Daddy,

I want you to know that you have made me the luckiest girl alive. I've never had anyone make me feel as special as you do. And nobody has ever come close to believing in me, and you show it to me every single day of our lives. I've yet to meet anyone who means more. I am so sure I understand why Mom married you. You are the greatest father in the world. I couldn't go to sleep tonight if I didn't write this down. You not only gave up your life, but you gave it up for us and you didn't just do a half job, because you never do half of anything. When people talk about their fathers, the greatest things they say never compare to even the slightest things you do. I feel strong when I see how you are a leader and lead by example. I want to be a follower of your path and I love you, Daddy. You are my best friend, my mom, everything I believe. Coming home to you makes everything I do important. I'm so lucky every day to be woken up by you."

SAVED

It happened on a Sunday when Mama was in the hospital. Sundays were always a good part of my childhood. I adored the feeling I got after leaving our church on a Sunday morning. Since we were little, my Mama insisted that we go to church every Sunday. We used to make it extraordinarily difficult. We would sit on the steps and kick and cry and scream that we did not want to get dressed. We complained at how boring it was. On top of that, we would pout the whole way there. No matter how miserable it must have been for Mama and Daddy, they took us every Sunday. I secretly began enjoying it.

Mama hadn't been able to attend the church services for many months. The different perfumes and colognes bothered her sensitive skin, and she would break out in rashes. Sometimes people would give us the altar flowers and a tape recording of the service for Mama to enjoy at the hospital. I had the altar flowers on my lap in the back seat of my Nan's Mercedes. We were headed home to change clothes before going to see Mama. I was staring out the window at a lush, green field, admiring the grass and wearing a light blue chiffon dress. Casey Kasem was hosting the Top 40 countdown on the radio.

Looking back at what I am about to tell you, it all makes sense. I can't know for certain, but I think Mama had been talking to Jesus often during cancer. I think she realized that she was not going to win this battle with cancer. And I imagine that she prayed for my brother and me. I think this was one of those times.

I sat silently observing the scenery when all of a sudden I felt a warm presence wash over my body. Nobody else in the car seemed to notice. Everything around me was fuzzy, and something above me was finely tuned. I instantly knew it was an angel. I remember having learned that every time you say a prayer, God assigns an angel to that prayer. I wondered if Mama had died and she was visiting me on her way to Heaven. I knew God had already created all of the angels that would ever exist. No, Mama couldn't be an angel. My body was weightless on the beige leather seat, and my eyes widened in obedience. The angel told me to be good. He gently told me that I could choose goodness. If I chose to be good, he ensured me that I would forever be taken care of. He didn't have to say by whom, I already knew. It was simple, and he left the choice up to me. He told me that God has placed much good in me and has something special planned for me. Yet the choice was mine to be good and believe in Him. I considered the proposition, and I said I choose to be good. I just kind of knew I would be good.

I have never been so alert, so in tune, so certain about anything. That angel was so pure and calm and provocative all at once. My little heart literally transformed itself that morning. God had put a song in my heart.

THE CEO

We always seemed to have our most important talks in the car. And we spent a lot of time in the car with Daddy, whether it was driving to our hundreds of practices or making the annual eighteen-hour trip to Florida. It was then that he had our full attention, as there was little option for us to be distracted or to walk away. He let us talk as much or as little as we wanted. We really bonded during times like these.

He would always tell us things about his day. He would tell us about the customers he saw or about the jobs he went on. He was open about everything, including his finances and such. He would tell us about our Pap or a family friend he saw at a grocery store. There is one lesson that stands out particularly bright in my memory.

My Daddy and Pap were well respected in their business. They made good money, but if you saw them on the street, you would never know it. I loved that they wore their blue service uniforms that were splattered with oil and grease. And my Daddy would often wear my brother's old blue and lime green Air Force Ones, which we thought was absolutely ridiculous. When we went on service calls with my Daddy, it was often to butcher shops, meat rooms, or grocery stores.

Whenever Daddy walked into a grocery store, all the employees knew him in every department. He would joke with each of them and ask about their families. I never took this for granted. I liked that they liked my Daddy. We always went grocery shopping after church on Sundays. I would wait in line at the deli counter and the sweet lady would always give me and my brother extra slices of cheese and lunch meat. She almost never charged us for the items we ordered. We waited there eating our slices of cheese, while Daddy was in the back calibrating a scale in his dress suit.

During the summer, we would ride our bikes to our favorite pizza shop in town, and the owner would never charge us for our pizza and sodas. When Pap was with us, we would tell him how nice that was. He always said, "Honey, he didn't give you that for free." I would ask what do you mean, and Pap would say, "Your Daddy's always doing favors for everyone! He owes us $500!" Pap would just laugh. I secretly was proud of Daddy for doing favors for his customers.

Daddy always told us that it was important every day, no matter what you were wearing or who you were with, to get to know the janitor and the CEO of the company. Everywhere you go, make sure you are humble enough to give the time of day to both. I always took Daddy's advice very seriously. He never steered me wrong.

HOME

At the hospital one afternoon, I remember overhearing Mama talking on the phone to her friend. I was doing a crossword puzzle on the bed next to Mama's. Mama said that all she wanted to do was go home. Naturally, I had expected Mama to wish to be able to go do something adventurous or go somewhere exotic. I had not expected that she would want to spend her numbered days at our home. Of all the places she had visited, of all the sites she had seen, noises she had heard, foods she had tasted, things she had touched, she wanted to be in our home — as a mother and wife.

Years later, I know exactly what she means.

Amanda M. Harding

The Woman of the House

Part Twelve
LIVING WITH LOSS

The Woman of the House

LIVING WITH LOSS

Living without a loved one is terribly difficult at times. It can send me into a fit of tears. I am grateful for the ability to share my story with others so that they can see there is hope to lead a fulfilling and genuine life. Your circumstances don't have to define you, but sometimes it's nice when they do!

UNLOVED

I've never felt unloved. In our house, I was the sun and my family the earth that revolved around me. I was the woman of the house. For as little recognition as women receive elsewhere in their lives, I witnessed a curious spectacle as I portrayed the center of a universe. The woman of the house is the pulse of the family. Where she goes, the family is sure to follow. Thus, it was my responsibility to keep the blood pumping, to keep my family moving forward, day by day.

I could choose to take on as little or as much responsibility as I wanted, or so it seemed. I was constantly reminded, during our counseling sessions, that I was not required nor expected to take my Mama's place. This sounded rosy and probably looked eloquent in a textbook, but its purpose never resonated with me. If not me, then who?

By God's grace, at the age of eighteen, I had already raised a father and a brother.

DADDY'S GIRL

I've always been more like my Daddy than my Mama. Most notably, I am a morning person. I am ridiculously self-motivated like my father. I remember my Daddy used to always make fun of my brother and Mama on the weekend mornings because we'd have washed our fleet of cars and taken batting practice before they even emerged from under their covers. Daddy and I love to travel. Sometimes, I wonder if by traveling I really mean unintentionally disappearing or running away from challenging things. I know that one day I will pick up on the drop of a dime and go on an adventure. Heads Carolina, tails California.

I liked Daddy's routines. When I was a little girl, Daddy used to go to McDonald's each morning and order a large coffee. One cream. One Equal. Then one day the lady who took his order every day, for as long as I could remember, told him that there was a study that showed Equal was known to cause cancer. From that day on, his ordered changed to one large coffee. One cream. One sugar. That was it. Recently, I had an aha moment when I caught myself at a McDonald's drive-through ordering a large iced coffee on my way to work. I'm so much like him sometimes.

I know Mama drank coffee because we still have the nice white coffee pot that Nan bought her one time for Christmas. I also remember when I was little and we were living in our old townhouse that she had put a coffee mug on my bedroom dresser. I must have knocked it over and steaming hot coffee spilled all over my baby brother. I remember she was screaming and called our pediatrician, and we had to put him into an icy bathtub.

One time a little girl at church told Daddy he had too much cologne on. So he completely stopped wearing it. I kind of missed the smell lingering in the hallway outside my bedroom in the morning, the indicator that he was already downstairs cooking us breakfast. I used to casually ask him if he needed more cologne because I never smelled it anymore. I miss that.

Whenever Daddy talked on the phone, he would grab a pen and paper nearby and draw these little tiny boxes that he would then draw diagonal lines through. I used to see those drawings on pieces of scrap paper in his work van, our kitchen, and his office desk. One day in college I caught myself drawing those boxes as the professor went on and on about something.

WILL

I never knew if Mama had actually written a will or not, but one day I was in the kitchen cleaning out the old Tupperware containers, trying to match each with its lid. Usually, when I emptied the dishwasher I threw them up there and wedged them in the cabinet until it would close. Daddy always told me to do it right because someone could get hurt opening it.

Well, I climbed up on the counter so I was eye level with the highest cabinet. There were some old bowls that we rarely ever used up there. I was feeling particularly motivated to clean that day. I wanted to start fresh, so I pulled everything out of the cabinet. I found a few pieces of paper folded into thirds.

Of course, I pulled them out and opened them. I have very little respect for other people's privacy sometimes, which still gets me into trouble. But our house was like a treasure chest. On any given day, I felt like I could go into a different place in the house and find something of Mama's that I had never known about before. Something to comfort me. Something to remind me that she really had existed and that she was always near.

The papers detailed where we were supposed to live if something ever happened to Mama or to Daddy or to both of them. I started feeling sick to my stomach, and I began crying loudly as I comprehended what this would mean. I did not want to live with anybody else. I would not live with anyone else. Even if I was only sixteen years old, I would raise my brother just fine. I was not going to live with some strange relative. Ever. And if I had to, I would make their lives a living hell. I ripped the papers up in my hand and flushed them down the toilet. In my fury, I was careful not to destroy Mama's signature. I kept that little piece of paper and put it somewhere in my desk drawer. I have never been able to find it since.

The Woman of the House

Part Thirteen

IF I COULD SAY ONE MORE THING

The Woman of the House

Amanda M. Harding

IF I COULD SAY ONE MORE THING

I was sitting outside on my patio this morning. We bought a house, you know. I am wearing my lavender snuggly bath robe. The birds are chirping. The cement is cool on my feet. The clouds are mingling with the sun in my favorite tones of sunrise. Our backyard is blooming, and the sweet scent of cut grass makes me nostalgic. I finished last night's dishes, so the kitchen is clean. That makes me happy.

I wish you were here. I wish you had called me last night while I was washing the dishes to ask me if you could come by to help me choose a paint color for the nursery. I wish my morning was like this . . .

You would let yourself in the front door and put two coffees and a bag of croissants that you picked up on your way over here on the patio table. You'd be wearing something new, your hair and

163

makeup already applied for the day. I'd catch a whiff of your perfume, and I would be glad you never changed scents. You would ask me how I was feeling and just grin at my belly. You'd tell me about my brother's and Daddy's latest adventure trying to get the boat started. We'd sit and talk and I wouldn't worry about anything I said. I'd catch a glimpse of your tan calves and realize how much mine resemble yours. You'd tell me you had a coupon for Jo-Ann's, and we could swing by there before going to look at paint. My husband would walk outside and kiss you and me good morning. You would smile as he kissed my belly. You would love him so dearly and think to yourself how happy you were that I found myself a Small Town Boy.

GOOGLE

Every so often when I am on the Internet at work, I will Google Mama's name. I'll try her maiden name and then her married name. I've never been able to find her obituary. I wonder if she published something that I don't know about, perhaps under a different name. So far, the best I can find is her name on a list of high school reunion blogs.

Amanda M. Harding

The Woman of the House

Part Fourteen

GOING FORWARD

The Woman of the House

GOING FORWARD

Browsing the blogosphere one day, I came across the term: post-traumatic growth.

"Post-traumatic growth refers to positive psychological change experienced as a result of the struggle with highly challenging life circumstances. Post-traumatic growth is not simply a return to baseline from a period of suffering; instead it is an experience of improvement that for some persons is deeply meaningful.

Individual differences in coping strategies set some people on a maladaptive spiral, whereas others proceed on an adaptive spiral. With this in mind, some early success in coping could be a precursor to posttraumatic growth. A person's level of confidence could also play a role in her or his ability to persist into growth or, out of lack of confidence, give up."

Perhaps this is what I've experienced. This is my story of post-traumatic growth. Becoming the woman of the house in a new household, breaking the bonds of my childhood role, was monumental for me. That I could live a normal life and was able to find a husband and raise a family of my own is powerful and proof that I do not have to hold onto guilt or limit myself because of what I've experienced.

I WAS THE WOMAN OF THE HOUSE

I was the woman of the house. I was given the task of raising my seven-year-old brother and forty-two-year-old father. I could propel them forward, sacrificing my youth at the chance to propel us all forward, or I could mess it up and hinder us. Truth be told, the latter option never proposed itself in my initial consideration. The choice was already spoken; I would make our home better than any home with a Mama in it.

If I am to be this heir, I would need to establish authority.

Later in life I would have the option to choose my family. I would only seek potential husbands whose parents were still married. It very much concerned me that I had no example of how a husband and wife interacted. I was playing a role all these years that excluded some major components. I trusted that if my future husband had been raised in a loving marriage that he could help me fill in the missing pieces. It was a must.

PREGNANCY

In her closet Mama kept shoe boxes, brown boxes, plastic boxes, and drawers full of pictures and undeveloped film spools. Sometimes I would find Mama in the middle of organizing the pictures into chronological order before placing each one into an album sleeve. The albums would be for us. She never finished, and so there are several boxes still in her closet.

In high school, while rummaging through her closet, I discovered a stack of Polaroids Mama had taken of herself in a bathroom mirror throughout her pregnancy with me. I hid them behind another picture that was already in an album so nobody would see. I've been taking the same sorts of pictures of my growing belly. I like to see how we compare.

THE FLOOD

Four months before we were to be married, Joe and I sat on the couch in Pastor Bill's office. We were required to complete a minimum of three premarital counseling sessions with Pastor Bill in order to be married at our church. I hadn't been to counseling since right after Mama's death, and I was actually looking forward to it. I thought I had the system figured out. We had gotten into a small disagreement earlier in the morning, and I was ready to talk. Well, I was sort of ready to get Joe to talk, and I had secretly hoped Pastor Bill would take my side on the disagreement, whatever it was.

Joe and I had recently found out that the offer we had made on our first home had been accepted. I had just started a new job, was planning a large wedding, doing paperwork for the house, and writing a book. Joe was working over sixty hours a week, taking five college classes, and putting up with me.

Pastor Bill had no agenda. He asked us how things were going in our lives, and we filled him in. We played our roles perfectly. And then we started talking about some of the issues we were having. One had to do with my Daddy. I had a tendency to consult with Daddy on everything, often times consulting with Daddy first and then relaying the decision to Joe. I knew this was wrong. Joe was to be the decision maker now. He was going to be the head of my household. That is what I wanted. But I was having a very difficult time "leaving and cleaving." Before I met Joe, Daddy was the only man in my life. He answered every question and was there for me any time I needed him. Literally, if I needed something, he would drop everything to make sure I had what I needed and/or wanted.

Joe and Pastor Bill were discussing the common issues and roles that parents play in every marriage. They were touching it delicately and appropriately. But my situation felt so different. Pastor Bill didn't know that Daddy was the only person I had. I did not have two parents. Daddy made sure I was safe at all times. He always knew what was best for me.

Daddy was both Mommy and Daddy for the greater part of my life. He had so much joy when my brother and I succeeded. We were what he invested his time into. Plain and simple, we were his life. I know Daddy was elated that I had found Joe. And I know that Daddy wants the best for us. I am so aware and appreciative of this.

However, sitting there on Pastor Bill's black pleather couch, I felt like something was overwhelming me. My eyes were watering up. Joe and Pastor Bill continued to talk casually while I was having a mental breakdown inside. All of a sudden, I hiccupped and the floodgates opened. I started bawling. The sweater I was wearing was making the back of my neck sweaty, and I had to readjust my hair. Pastor Bill stopped talking for a moment, and they both just stared at me. I couldn't keep my composure. I just kept crying. Pastor Bill reached onto his bookshelf and handed me a wad of Kleenex. I held it up to my eyes and let it sop up the tears that would not cease. I attempted to envision the bottle of purple nail polish with the black wand floating in front of me, but I guess that tear blocker is only good for a one-and-done deal.

Pastor Bill was trying to take hold of the unexpected scene. When it was apparent that I could not talk between my sobs, Pastor Bill filled the silence by asking Joe if he knew what the matter was. Joe looked amused, concerned, and sad, and I saw tears in his eyes too. I knew he would know. He calmly said that he thought I might be upset because of my Mama and because she had passed away when I was twelve. They both looked at me, and I started crying harder in response to the accuracy of his statements. I tried staring at the grout lines on the tile floor. Anything. Pastor Bill nodded in understanding. He understood the part of me that was missing. Of all the things I could have used for the few words I would muster, I simply squeezed out the correction that, no she died when I was ten. And then I continued to sob into my Kleenex for the remaining hour of our session. Pastor Bill tried telling me an array stories and personal experiences in an attempt to cheer me up, but he didn't know what button he had hit. I only cried harder.

In a subsequent session, we determined that I was feeling anxiety about cutting the cord from my father. The switch to having Joe as my leader now. It was a lot to take in, but I valued and respected marriage, and so this was very important for me to "get." I knew Joe was the one I wanted to lead me as my husband and me as his wife. Yet it was so hard to actually feel and recognize the shift this would create in my relationship with my Daddy. I was just heartbroken at the thought of what it meant for both me and my Daddy. He never let me down, not once.

WITH OR WITHOUT HER

After cancer, it was like an expired hourglass was flipped in my heart, and thoughts of eventually having to fend entirely for myself were the little bits of sand pouring down on me. Year after year, the glass grew heavy.

I constantly asked myself the question, "If ___ were gone, would I still succeed in life?" For instance, I would fill in the blank with Daddy. If Daddy were gone, would I still have the tools and skills to finish college, raise my brother, and fulfill all of the other high expectations I had set for myself and my family. I always tweaked and justified my response until the answer was yes.

I always look at the bigger picture of my actions. I try to envision the trickle-down effect of how a certain decision will either help or hinder me in the future. If I don't want to see it on the front page of the newspaper, I won't do it.

I look at everything through that perspective. When my friends still had their childlike innocence, I would chastise them for not realizing how they were relying on so many other people to fulfill their happiness. I could never fathom the thought of letting a man do everything. In fact, that entire concept horrified me. What if your husband passed away and you were left with five children? Would you know how to mow the lawn, change the oil, or do other traditionally male-centered roles? Of course, I would think to myself that you would learn it eventually, but the thought of not being self-sufficient made me cringe. For as optimistic as my heart was at times, my head could be equally pessimistic.

I always knew that one day something, or someone, would flip that weighty hourglass over on its side where it was not infinitely showering down on me. Instead, it would lie still in perfect harmony.

That something, or someone, *is* God.

BRIDAL SHOWER

About a month before our wedding, Joe and I went up to his parent's house for the weekend. When we arrived at the house, I noticed the front yard was full of cars. I thought nothing of this since he is one of eleven children and has over forty nieces and nephews. I always have a bundle of nerves before visiting my in-laws. So I followed my husband inside. We were greeted by my future mother-in-law and about thirty other women. I choked up as I noticed pink-and-white decorations scattered throughout the house. There was food, and there were tablecloths, candles in decorated vases, flowers floating in crystal bowls, and pictures of my husband and me hanging like garland. My lips visibly trembled and my eyes watered as I fanned myself desperately to gain composure.

Here I was, motherless, at my bridal shower, hosted by the women who would soon become my family. I marvel at God's grace, at how He took my Mama from me so early in life, yet perfect in His timing, and delivered on His vow to stay near to me, by replacing my loss exponentially with a room full of Godly women and mothers. Women who serve not only as family but as examples for me of love, marriage, friendship, and motherhood.

It was Mother's Day 2012.

The Woman of the House

Part Fifteen

MOVING ON

The Woman of the House

THANKFUL

I will never get to know my Mama as a friend. She was not there to help me pick out my gown and plan my wedding. She was not there to hold my daughter. She will never give me her favorite recipes or call me to take me out to lunch. I will not know who her first kiss was or what her favorite book was. I will never be able to call her when I am upset or just want to talk. My children will not know the pure, unconditional love of their grandmother. She will not give me advice on decorating my first home or help me pick out furniture. I will not know how she found God.

But I do know that she is in heaven, and I will see her again one day. And I do know that she left me with a wonderful, loving father and brother. A father and brother whom I know not only as family but as best friends, who will hold my children, who helped me plan my wedding, who taught me how to cook on the grill and eat hard-shell crabs, who take me out to dinner for every birthday and bring me flowers for no reason at all, who I call when I am upset or when I am thrilled beyond belief. Who helped me move in and out of countless apartments and helped me furnish my first house, who were at every graduation, ceremony, recital, concert, and sporting event. I have a father who taught me how to earn an honest living and look a coach in the eye. I have a father who provided me with a loving home and childhood memories so sweet and wonderful that I can only hope to recreate such moments with my own children.

So, you see, I am blessed. I am blessed beyond measure.

Amanda M. Harding

The Woman of the House

EPILOGUE

Today is the 5,357th day I've lived without my Mama. The reality of time reveals itself to me in myriad ways. The birth of my own daughter, fifteen years after cancer, was life changing. I am so grateful for the opportunity to be a mother. So much so, that the day I finished this book I quit my lucrative job to become a stay at home Mama. I don't want to miss a second.

The Woman of the House

Amanda M. Harding

PSALM 91

He who dwells in the secret place of the Most High
Shall abide under the shadow of the Almighty.
I will say of the LORD, *"He is* my refuge and my fortress;
My God, in Him I will trust."

Surely He shall deliver you from the snare of the fowler
And from the perilous pestilence.
He shall cover you with His feathers,
And under His wings you shall take refuge;
His truth *shall be your* shield and buckler.
You shall not be afraid of the terror by night,
Nor of the arrow *that* flies by day,
Nor of the pestilence *that* walks in darkness,
Nor of the destruction *that* lays waste at noonday.

A thousand may fall at your side,
And ten thousand at your right hand;
But it shall not come near you.
Only with your eyes shall you look,
And see the reward of the wicked.

Because you have made the LORD, *who is* my refuge,
Even the Most High, your dwelling place,
No evil shall befall you,
Nor shall any plague come near your dwelling;
For He shall give His angels charge over you,
To keep you in all your ways.
In *their* hands they shall bear you up,
Lest you dash your foot against a stone.
You shall tread upon the lion and the cobra,
The young lion and the serpent you shall trample underfoot.

"Because he has set his love upon Me, therefore I will deliver him;
I will set him on high, because he has known My name.
He shall call upon Me, and I will answer him;
I *will be* with him in trouble;
I will deliver him and honor him.
With long life I will satisfy him,
And show him My salvation."

The Woman of the House

33925925R20120

Made in the USA
Charleston, SC
27 September 2014